I0149656

INVISIBLE

GOD'S LOVING PURSUIT OF HIS UNSEEN DAUGHTERS

BRENDA ERB ROBERTS

ISBN: 978-1-4866-2451-5
eBook ISBN: 978-1-4866-2452-2

Word Alive Press
119 De Baets Street Winnipeg, MB R2J 3R9
www.wordalivepress.ca

WORD ALIVE
—P R E S S—

Cataloguing in Publication information can be obtained from Library and Archives Canada.

"Invisible: God's Loving Pursuit of His Unseen Daughters is a book of encouragement for any woman who has felt ashamed, insignificant, overlooked, and neglected. Through bringing to life the stories of women in the Bible and applying their experiences to modern life with humour, Erb Roberts describes the relentless pursuit of God to love, honour, and restore his daughters. Don't stay stuck. Read this book and begin your journey to step out of the shadows."

—Grant W. Mullen, M.D.
Author of *Emotionally Free*

"Brenda Erb Roberts nailed it. *Invisible: God's Loving Pursuit of His Unseen Daughters* is a book that you will not be able to put down.

With thought, imagination, and emotion, Brenda, takes her readers on a journey through the Bible to encounter the stories of 13 women. Using humor and fresh, relatable examples, Brenda reminds us that feelings of invisibility are common and were experienced both in biblical times and today. Yet God's creative plan directs the narrative of our lives to showcase His love for His unseen daughters no matter what era they live in, or what circumstances they find themselves in.

You will laugh. You will cry. You will deeply reflect on the wonder of God and His amazing workings on behalf of His chosen daughters. This book belongs in your hands."

—Margaret Gibb
Founder and Executive Director, Women Together

"Many women have felt this way at one time or another...*felt* being the key word. Yes, feelings have a way of usurping what's true. How we feel or how we are made to feel due to our circumstances can pull us into a pit of despair.

Brenda Erb Roberts has beautifully scripted the stories of thirteen kindred hearts that felt invisible, that were rescued by their creator and persuaded that not only were they seen, but intimately known, and fiercely loved.

You will be drawn into their pain, their frustration, their desperation, their aloneness, and fear.

You will see yourself, and ultimately, you will see your God and like your thirteen sisters be completely overwhelmed by the truth that you are indeed, a Beloved Daughter."

—Sue Keddy
President, Dream Big With Us

"Invisible: God's Loving Pursuit of His Unseen Daughters" by Brenda Erb Roberts is designed to help women see themselves as God sees them—as dearly beloved daughters. It unpacks the relatable stories of women who found, down through the ages, in the middle of their difficulties, that God was faithful. Each of us has baggage; this book helps us to understand that God can use those things that the enemy intended for our destruction and make them work for our good and His glory. Allow this book to speak hope to your heart."

—Tony denBok
Lead Pastor, Clearview Community Church

"Brenda Erb Roberts has put together an inspirational book using several women in the Bible as examples to us. It is wonderful how she shares her own heart on feeling invisible at times in her life while expounding on the blessings and love of God despite our inadequacies."

—Denise Mountenay
Author of *The Bride, The Serpent & The Seed*
Speaker/Filmmaker, Together for Life Ministries

To my beloved daughter, Kirstin, and beloved daughter-in-law, Emily.
May you find your voices earlier in life than I did
and use them to sing from the rooftops.

CONTENTS

INTRODUCTION

I am not invisible. It seemed like such a simple concept. One that any six-year-old would understand. But she wasn't six, and it wasn't simple. That revelation was life-changing, and it rocked her world.

Health issues had sidelined her, and her life had deteriorated into a series of shoulds and have-tos. The highlight of some days was a rousing game of "Seek and Destroy the Dust Bunnies" before diving into her stimulating scullery maid duties—while life carried on for everyone else. Did anyone know her essence, she wondered, or did they only see the results of her drudgery? She felt as if she didn't matter. As if she were invisible. Being invisible would be a superpower; feeling invisible was not.

And then she had an epiphany—it was as if a lightning bolt illuminated a truth that exploded like fireworks in her soul. A new understanding of the Bible story about Jesus' baptism overwhelmed her. Matthew 3:16–17 says:

> And when Jesus was baptized, immediately he went up from the water, and behold, the heavens were opened to him, and he saw the Spirit of God descending like a dove and coming to rest on him; and behold, a voice from heaven said, "This is my *beloved Son*, with whom I am well pleased." (emphasis added)

Long ago, she had chosen to become a follower of Christ and part of God's family, his child. If she was a child of God, it must be true that she was also his beloved daughter. Not just one member of a vast family but a *Beloved Daughter*. And that is when her world changed. *I am not invisible!*

That woman was me.

With that new awareness of my identity, I turned to my Bible and discovered I wasn't alone; its pages contained stories about women who had also felt invisible. Ultimately, they too learned that they were Beloved Daughters.

Based on conversations with kindred spirits, I've learned that the struggle with feelings of invisibility isn't limited to Bible times or me. In our society, though the circumstances and stage of life may differ from person to person, a quiet cry resides in the heart of many women: *Please, see me.*

If that's how you feel, let me encourage you. God knows you intimately, and he values you. You are not invisible to him. Matthew 10:29–31 says:

> Are not two sparrows sold for a penny? And not one of them will fall to the ground apart from your Father? But even the hairs of your head are all numbered. Fear not, therefore; you are of more value than many sparrows.

Women in the Bible have travelled this path before us. If you think one needed to be the poster child of a virtuous woman to have her story recorded in the pages of scripture, think again. The women whose lives we'll delve into in this book were not perfect. Some were unremarkably ordinary, others notorious, but they all required help. From their narratives, I've learned how our loving heavenly Father pursued them and how much he cared about them, their circumstances, and their deep wounds. And while learning about their lives, I was reminded how much God cares about me. Preserved through many generations, these accounts of troubled and suffering women reveal God's heart to us.

Unfortunately, our world doesn't look much different from this ancient society. Many troubled and suffering women still need help. The good news is that the same God who aided these women in their plights can do the same for you and me. He hasn't changed. The Bible assures us that *"Jesus Christ is the same yesterday and today and forever"* (Hebrews 13:8), so we may safely put our confidence in him. That message encourages me, and I hope it encourages you as well.

I've taken some liberties with the biblical accounts and included fictitious details to add colour and bring their stories to life. But each one describes a real woman living in an actual situation, and I haven't altered the truths portrayed in the text.

One woman lived a life of quiet desperation, invisible to her world because she'd been bleeding for twelve years and was worse after being "helped" by many doctors. In faith, she touched Jesus' clothes, and her life took a whole new track—no gynecological exam required. Learn how Jesus gave a new identity and health to someone hidden on the sidelines of life.

Sarah had issues. She couldn't produce an heir for her husband, even though God promised it would happen. So feeling abandoned and unseen, this disappointed wife enacted a brilliant scheme to have her servant Hagar become her surrogate. Unfortunately, the strategy spectacularly backfired, because she couldn't make God's plan happen without God's help. See how this train wreck was redeemed when God stepped in, and witness the remarkable legacy that resulted despite her harebrained idea.

Hagar, Sarah's servant, became a surrogate mother for her employer, only to have that same employer turn on her and expel her from her home. Well, that's the short version. Hagar contributed to the problem, which makes her a lot like us. Alone, feeling forsaken, and in a terrible predicament, God pursued her and sent angels to her rescue twice. Enter her world and see how her tale of woe doesn't have many woes left once a loving God reaches out to her.

Rahab was a lady with a less-than-stellar past—a prostitute, a shadow-dweller with a low profile, and an unlikely candidate for an ancestor of Jesus. Read her narrative and delight in how God saw, pursued, and dramatically rescued her from a life-threatening situation and how he rewarded this Beloved Daughter for her faith despite the label she wore. Watch God's grace unfold in her story and see her impressive family tree as a testament to it.

Naomi and Ruth experienced more than their fair share of misery in life. This mother-in-law and daughter-in-law were a remarkable pair. Both were widows; the older woman had also lost her two sons, while the younger was childless when her husband died. But through an unusual story of love and devotion, we watch God pull all the pieces of their sad lives together and create something new and beautiful. Join this indomitable pair of Beloved Daughters on their journey and see how God orchestrated a rescue like no other for them. And—spoiler alert—he even threw in a romantic love story as a bonus. How great is that?

Hannah and another woman shared the same husband. The other wife could bear children, but Hannah couldn't, making her feel invisible and less than a wife should be in her culture. However, their husband loved Hannah more than his other wife. If you think that's a set-up for good times, think again. The other wife made life pure misery for Hannah. Dip into her saga and see how God heard and acted on behalf of this formerly invisible woman, his Beloved Daughter.

Leah and Rachel were two sisters whose Dear Old Dad duped them into becoming sister wives. Leah was older, not a knockout, and unmarried, and Daddy traded her for her gorgeous sister, Rachel, on the wedding night. Revolted by the switch, Hubby Jacob protested vehemently to his father-in-law and then married the coveted Rachel a week later. Ever after this, Leah the Unattractive was Leah the Invisible because Jacob had never loved her in the first place. Although their husband loved her, Rachel struggled with infertility and her own battle with invisibility. Discover how God saw and pursued each of them individually, offering help and hope to his Beloved Daughters.

Martha and Mary were another set of sisters with very different personalities and their own invisibility issues. Martha was the do-it-all type who was stressed and frayed, unseen in the kitchen as she attempted to entertain Jesus in the style to which she was accustomed. As you may expect, she was grumpy when her sister didn't support her efforts. Mary was the quiet one, hidden in the background, and appeared to be the slacker. Delve into their narrative and be encouraged regardless of which role resonates with you. Jesus' eyes were on both of them, and he loved each one as a Beloved Daughter, despite any shortcomings.

A woman with a tarnished reputation, whose lifestyle relegated her to the fringes of society, and another who became invisible as a person when her flagrant sin defined her, were surprisingly not condemned by Jesus. After they encountered him, they didn't slink away and remain invisible. They flew out of his presence with their heads held high, forgiven, and with a story to tell. Travel the path to hope with these two women and bask in the wonder that Jesus didn't require them to be paragons of virtue before he invited them to become Beloved Daughters. I don't think any of us would qualify if that were the stipulation.

You may be fortunate and have never felt unseen or unknown. Even so, your daughter, sister, mother, or friend may struggle this way. Or maybe you aren't old enough to have experienced those feelings—yet. Whatever your circumstances, I pray that God will speak to you through these women's lives.

My story is one of redemption, like each woman in this book. When you feel like the girl serving punch at the prom rather than dancing the night away, be assured: God sees you. He revealed the truth in these narratives to me when I felt utterly alone and unseen. Although many of my circumstances remain the same, my perspective has changed. I know that I am a Beloved Daughter. And I always will be.

I invite you to join me and begin your own journey of discovery. Prepare to be astounded by how this loving God helped some invisible damsels in distress and ushered them into the realm of Beloved Daughters.

At the back of this book is a section titled "Let's Get Personal." Here you can dig deeper into the stories and concepts discussed. It lists the scripture passages for each chapter and contains questions designed for self-reflection, group discussion, journaling, or sharing with a trusted friend.

Rest assured, you are not alone—we're sisters on this pathway together, and there is someone who sees each of us and loves us dearly. So let the adventure begin!

"Cast your burden on the Lord, and he will sustain you ..." (Psalm 55:22).

1

FROM PATIENT TO BELOVED
—THE HEMORRHAGING WOMAN

Picture yourself sitting in a doctor's office, trying to appear calm as you wait to consult with her about a potentially significant medical issue, or squirming while you anticipate test results you hope won't crash your world. Been there? I have. Imagine your desperation if no doctor, specialist, or alternative medicine practitioner has been able to put an end to your suffering, and you're feeling worse than when your troubles began. And now, at the end of your financial resources, you learn that this doctor, your final hope, can't help. Would you feel invisible? Would you feel as though your life didn't matter to anyone? I know I would.

The story of the hemorrhaging woman—from the biblical books of Matthew, Mark and Luke—about a lady with a chronic health condition begins this way, but it doesn't end there. Let's explore how an encounter with Jesus transported a disheartened woman from a life of invisibility and misery to a Beloved Daughter and see what we can learn from her experience.

A crowd of people fidget, like children at the mailbox anticipating a gift but not knowing when it will arrive. The tension is palpable as they listen for Jesus' approaching footsteps, the murmur of chatter and the irritating drone of flies heavy in the air. They wait. Each one is there for their own reasons. Some have physical needs beyond physicians' ability to treat, while others struggle with dire situations that only a miracle from heaven can resolve. Some just crave a glimpse of the man who had set the Twitterverse of the day on fire.

Now observe one particular woman jostled in the crush of sweating bodies, breathing the pungent and dusty air, wilting from the heat of the blazing sun beating on her head. She shuffles from foot to foot as her anticipation and anxiety build. For twelve long years, she has been bleeding, and it has been gruelling. With its magical surgeries to address such problems, today's Western medicine isn't an option for her, and every woman in our era can sympathize. Her life is a mess. With each passing month, then year, that her ordeal continues, hope drifts further and further from her grasp, and disappointment threatens to extinguish even a glimmer of it. The twilight world of "If only …" envelopes her. It's as if she's living on the outside of life, peering through a window but never crossing the threshold. Her life is on perpetual hold as she awaits that moment when it will be feasible to dream again, to truly live again.

Countless doctors have treated her, and now she's at the end of her medical journey looking at a dismal future. Since universal Medicare or private insurance aren't part of her world, her bank account is empty. Long ago, she used her investments to cover the cost of the elusive cures she chased, and now her condition is worse than when she first sought help.[1] As a result of losing so much blood, she's probably also anemic, compounding her problem. Chances are, her identity has gradually morphed from a person, a wife, a mother, or a friend, into a patient. With her pursuit of a medical solution at an end, she doesn't even have

---

[1] Mark 5:26.

that label to stick on her robe anymore. She needs help desperately, and aside from a miracle, there's nowhere else to turn.

Can you imagine how wretched and life-sucking her experience would have been? This lady was not only sick but probably lonely too. The relentless drive to find relief devoured her time, energy, and resources. If you've ever bounced from one specialist to another, you understand how draining the search for help is, regardless of the toll the illness takes on your body. The limitations imposed by her condition would have prevented her participation in numerous activities, and many friends would have drifted away as their paths diverged. Their lives had moved on; hers had not. It would have been a terrible trap. No matter how hard she tried, she couldn't fully participate in the life she had formerly known.

Alone in her struggle, she seems like the poster child for invisibility. Just one in a drove of people, many as desperate as she, all hoping to intercept Jesus, she continues to wait. But somehow, even though ill, she has reached the place where an encounter with Jesus could happen.

Do you know what stuns me? She hadn't given up but was sardined in a mob of other seekers, awaiting Jesus' attention. After all of her suffering, this action reveals her belief that she wasn't beyond rescuing and that she still had hope for a cure. She didn't cope by eating popcorn on the couch and watching soap operas, or the equivalent in her day, in the hope of soothing her distress. No, she was packed in the excited throng, awaiting her moment with Jesus.

Then, a cloud of dust appears in the distance as a tiny figure unhurriedly comes into view and inches his way toward the expectant hopefuls. A cheer erupts from the mass—Jesus is coming!—and he is coming to them. And then, she is *scooped*.

Have you ever waited and waited until your turn finally arrived, only to have someone jump in ahead of you and steal your moment? It's not fun. The epic scoop in my life occurred the night I became engaged to my husband. My older sister had married her childhood sweetheart at twenty, but I waited longer for my handsome prince. Eventually, my Prince Charming found me. The evening he proposed seemed enchanted, with the question posed on bended knee, the presentation of the ring, and then dinner at a magnificent dining establishment—the kind where you can't afford to eat after you're married. One of those evenings you fantasized about when you were a little girl, and one you remember in all its lovely details forty years later.

Then came the scoop. Excitedly, I phoned my parents to tell them what I perceived to be earth-shaking news, thinking they would be delighted. For years they'd been hoping I'd find the right man, and were possibly afraid I never would. My mother's response was, "That's nice. Your sister had a baby tonight." In all fairness, my mother was never at her best at night, and the call was past her usual bedtime. And unbeknownst to me, my fiancé had asked my father's permission in advance, so our engagement didn't spark the level of surprise and excitement I had anticipated. Regardless, I remember feeling deflated by my mother's response to my announcement. My sister hadn't scheduled the birth of her baby (her third daughter) to eclipse my news, but a new grandchild proved to be an exceedingly hard act to follow.

Being scooped would feel significantly worse if your health and future well-being were at stake. Finally, after she's waited for ages in the vast throng, the man of the hour arrives and is within reach. All of her efforts to get to the right place at the right time to have a chance at a healthy life are about to pay off. Then Jairus, an important man in the religious world, somehow manoeuvres to the front of the crowd, throws himself at Jesus' feet, and begs him to come to his house. His only daughter is dying. Will Jesus please heal her? Yes, he will. And the man who embodies hope turns to accompany Jairus home.[2] With that gesture, the possibility of an encounter with the only person who can make the hemorrhaging woman whole and give her a blessedly ordinary life is in danger of evading her.

It's excellent news for Jairus that Jesus will visit his home. The Lord doesn't ask that distraught father to bring his sick daughter to him but is willing to make the journey himself. But is it great news for the others who've also been waiting? Imminent death is a compelling reason to push to the front of the line, and I can't imagine the hemorrhaging woman begrudging Jairus aid for such a grave plight. Still, after waiting so long for assistance, it's another roadblock to receiving the relief she

....
[2] Mark 5:22–24.

seeks, possibly an insurmountable obstacle if an opportunity to connect with Jesus never again arises.

In her circumstances, I may have turned away with a broken heart and tears streaming down my face, thinking my last option had vanished. Not this lady. Even though she'd been bleeding for twelve years, she hadn't given up and wasn't about to wither in defeat now. She accepts the challenge and devises an alternate plan. However, this is an invisible woman, and the course of action she chooses reveals that the spotlight is far from her comfort zone.

Little by little, inch by inch, she worms her way through the horde of people, focused on her mission. Anyone in her wake notices her deliberate movements, and no one stops her from reaching Jesus. The expression on her face indicates that she's intent on achieving her goal despite being scooped by Jairus. She may have lived in the background for years, but despite being invisible, this lady has grit, which the *Canadian Oxford Dictionary* defines as "pluck, endurance, strength of character."[3] Health issues have threatened to crush her, but she refuses to be powerless. Determination combined with grit and faith gives her the strength to execute the coup of a lifetime.

At long last, the lady is within reach of the one who holds the key to her future. After successfully fighting through the sea of bodies, the critical moment arrives. Extending her hand is a gesture that has never before held such consequence. Does she tremble as fear and anticipation grip her? In the attempt to touch Jesus' clothes, because this desperate soul knows even that will be enough to heal her,[4] she connects with one of the tassels on the corner of his shawl[5] as it swings while he walks.[6] With

....

[3] The Canadian Oxford Dictionary, 2nd ed., s.v. "Grit, n."

[4] Mark 5:28.

[5] The hemorrhaging woman crawling on the ground to touch the bottom hem of Jesus' garment is a deeply moving picture of an invisible woman. But many commentaries, like *Luke: An Introduction and Commentary* by Leon Morris, explain that the woman touched "the tassel on the end of the square garment that was thrown over the left shoulder and hung down the back (Num. 15:38ff.). We should not think of the lower hem, as this could not be reached in the circumstances" (Morris, *Luke*, 178).

[6] Luke 8:44.

that fleeting contact, this woman's life changes forever. The gesture is so discreet it's unlikely anyone in the vicinity even notices what she has done, which speaks so clearly of her invisibility. No friend is by her side to ask, "Did anything happen?" She is alone in her quest, but in an instant, her world hasn't just capsized but turned right side up. With great certainty, she knows she is healed, and Jesus knows it too.

Can you imagine what that instant felt like for her? Maybe she froze in amazement that her desperate venture to garner help worked. Perhaps deep joy unlocked a room within her soul that had harboured the heartbreak, disappointment, and overwhelming sadness she had felt for years and released them. A flood of quiet tears may have brushed her cheeks as she realized the enormity of what had happened. Or it could be that the amazed woman was just momentarily breathless. The Bible doesn't describe her initial response, but it records the result of her action—her ailing body was fixed, normal again, instantly.[7] Normal seems like such a bland word, but having coped with an abnormal body for so many years, normal would feel like Christmas and her birthday rolled into one, overlaid with a symphony playing at full volume. This moment would become one of those defining events in life where everything occurred either *before* or *after* it. Before—she was hemorrhaging; after—she was well. This healing would become a clear dividing line between two parts of her life, with no gray area between them.

And then, her quiet life of invisibility comes to a screeching halt. Probably not the way she would prefer, but end it most certainly does. Jesus immediately stops. He knows someone touched him, and not the kind of touch that would normally happen in a crowd when someone jostled him.[8] This touch was very distinctive. The great healer puts all his plans on hold while he pursues the person he seeks. When he asks who has touched him, not a soul admits it. Peter says it's a ridiculous question because there's an enormous, bustling crowd around him, and anyone could have bumped him. Insistent that someone has touched him in

[7] Luke 8:44.

[8] Luke 8:45.

6

a way that released power from him, Jesus demands an answer.[9] The intensity and tone of his voice may have unsettled the mass of onlookers, causing them to wonder what is about to happen.

The culprit desperately attempts to remain unnoticed in the background and is shaking in her sandals, quite literally,[10] because there is no way out. Jesus had asked a direct question, and he expects an honest answer. The authority in his voice brooks no hedging. Having spent the last twelve years living an inconspicuous life, the invisible woman suddenly has to step forward and publicly take responsibility for her action. What's going through her mind? Does she want the ground to open and swallow her? Or is her first thought to bolt away from the crowd as fast as she can to return to her quiet life, albeit in a much better state of health? Well, she makes an honourable choice. Unable to remain invisible, she finds her voice, makes herself known to Jesus, and falls in front of him.

Confessing in front of a crowd that she is the one who touched him and was healed by doing so is excruciating enough, but it gets worse. When she raises her head to speak to Jesus, she is acutely aware that she's not alone but in the company of a lot of *men*. Scores of men are part of the immense throng of people surrounding Jesus, and in that culture, an issue as private as she experienced isn't discussed in public, and certainly not in front of men. It's not a community where people walk around on the beach wearing clothing they only pretend covers their bodies, or where every type of personal product ever conceived is blatantly advertised. It's a society that highly values modesty. She needs to break some very ingrained rules of social behaviour to tell Jesus she'd been bleeding for twelve years—and not from her ears or nose. While that kind of bleeding wouldn't have been good, it would have been visible and appreciably less embarrassing. The fact that she openly shares her sad tale shows that she digs deeply and accesses her resources of courage and grit.

Having given Jesus a gut-wrenching account of her life after he so adamantly demanded to know who had taken healing power from him,

---

[9] Luke 8:45–46.

[10] Luke 8:47.

is she terrified of how he will react? Will he be angry or rescind the healing because she dared to touch him without permission? Is she in more trouble now than when she arrived? It isn't hard to empathize with her because she has no idea how he will respond.

Cringing in fear, she is conceivably expecting a backlash like, "Lady! What were you thinking?" However, Jesus doesn't respond that way. Any trace of apprehension or insecurity rattling inside her has to vanish when he speaks. *"Daughter"* is the first word he utters,[11] and I imagine a collective sigh escaping from the crowd, relieved they're not about to witness a train wreck. Jesus has pursued her and is on her side. She isn't invisible to him; he sees her. He uses "Daughter" as a proper noun, a name, giving her an identity. This lady who has been through so much is no longer just a patient or even an ex-patient. Rather than treating her as a trespasser who has stolen something precious from him, he addresses her as *family*. Awestruck, standing in front of Jesus, her universe shifts as she is transformed from an invisible woman to a Beloved Daughter. The invisible becomes visible to Jesus.

He proceeds beyond merely recognizing her but commends her and says her faith has made her well. It wasn't wishful thinking or the fact that she had a genuine need. It wasn't even her abject desperation. Her faith in Jesus, before whom she now stands, has made her body whole. He doesn't discharge her from his presence by returning to his business because countless people, including Jairus, await his attention. Instead, he chooses to convey a blessing rather than dismiss her. With the words, *"go in peace, and be healed of your disease,"*[12] Jesus releases her. No misplaced guilt for having stolen her healing, or shame for a condition that made her untouchable, will stalk her. She is emancipated—free from the bondage of an illness that held her hostage for far too long.

The power of a blessing can have lifelong ramifications. A friend shared the story of her grandmother's deathbed blessing, which she received when she was about fifteen. The grandmother, whom she dearly loved, and who had a substantial influence on my friend's life, was in the

---

[11] Mark 5:34.

[12] Mark 5:34b.

hospital near the end of her life. My friend believed this would be their last visit, and as she turned to leave her grandmother's room, Grandma stopped her and asked her to return to the bedside. She then imparted these words, which my friend has carried with her ever since: "I want you to know you always brought me nothing but joy." It was their last visit, and those were her grandmother's final words.

What potency there is in words. My friend's first thought was, *I've done something right.* To hear that affirmation at fifteen years of age would undoubtedly be one of those before-and-after moments we discussed, a line drawn in the sand of her life. Of course, her grandmother's blessing didn't eliminate all the struggles of her teen years and beyond, but she had those words to hold and cherish as her life unfolded. *Grandma loved me, and I was important to her.*

When I heard that story, I got chills down my back, and in re-telling it now, there are tears in my eyes. If we dared to act upon the declaration in Proverbs 18:21a—"*Death and life are in the power of the tongue*"—the impact we could have on the lives of those around us is astonishing.

After receiving healing and a blessing, the formerly hemorrhaging woman doesn't magically enter a fairyland where all her problems suddenly evaporate. Having lived in social isolation for so long, this lady may have lost touch with many friends and family. Besides, due to her medical expenses, she may have been living in reduced circumstances, if not abject poverty. Jesus releases her from the prison of ill health and changes her life, but there isn't a utopia awaiting her on the other side.

That's how real life works because if it didn't, we'd no longer need the one who frees us in the first place. The good news is that he doesn't abandon her, and he doesn't abandon us. He will walk with us through the following steps and the next. He isn't a fairy who touches us with a magic wand now and again to fix whatever's wrong and then flies away. He's in it with us for the long term.

This Daughter will need time and effort to re-establish relationships, and doing so will be a process rather than an instant occurrence. While not necessarily a formidable task, it's likely a bit daunting and includes much uncertainty. There's an expression that says, "You can't go home again." You understand this statement if you've been away for an extended period and long to go home and find things precisely as you left them. Things change. Time moves on, and people's lives don't stay static. The situation you remember doesn't exist in the same way anymore, so you must find a way to fit in again. That's her challenge, but with the grit she's already evidenced, I'm sure she can overcome it.

Have you ever felt like you were walking a path alone, invisible, much like the woman in this story, and no one understood what was happening in your life? Or if they did, they didn't know how to help, which seemed to translate in your mind to not caring? Let me encourage you. There is hope for you and me. David wrote many psalms in the Bible that are relatable even today because he struggled with the same feelings we do. Psalm 31:7 says, "*I will rejoice and be glad in your steadfast love, because you have seen my affliction; you have known the distress of my soul.*"

Rest assured—you are not invisible, and like the woman in this chronicle whose problem seemed insurmountable until she met Jesus, he is on your side! You are his Beloved Daughter, as am I, and he sees and loves you—or you *can* be if you haven't begun your journey with him yet. Isn't that fantastic? If you'd like to join his family and take your place as a Beloved Daughter, I encourage you to flip to the back of this book and read the section titled "How to Become a Follower of Christ." You will be eternally grateful you did.

2

From Dried Up Like a Prune to Beloved—Sarah

You've probably heard someone say, "Getting old sucks" or "Getting old isn't for sissies." These sentiments may be true for people struggling with any of the numerous challenges associated with aging, but one issue today's women generally don't have to deal with is having a baby at ninety years of age. Welcome to Sarah's world. As unbelievable as it may seem, this was her reality. But the path to reaching that state was anything but straight. Her narrative has more twists and turns than a narrow mountain road.

Sarah felt invisible and abandoned by the God who'd promised she would have a son. This disheartened woman then made an unwise decision that affected not only herself but another person. Yet despite the disaster she set in motion, God still loved, saw, and pursued her, and he honoured her faith in a remarkable way.

If you feel like God is missing in action somewhere and you're invisible or concerned that you've made a collosal, irredeemable mistake, explore Sarah's odyssey with me. She leaves the world of invisibility—in which her role is not what she and her husband desire—and embraces her identity as a Beloved Daughter. The end of her story will encourage you.

Before we discuss Sarah's plight, let's briefly examine her backstory to lay the foundation for her struggle. In the beginning, her name is Sarai, and she's married to Abram, who later becomes Abraham.[13] God calls Abram to leave his home and follow him to an undisclosed location somewhere in the great beyond. The details Abram receives are extremely vague, but these are the elements:

- Pack up and follow me, and I will create a great nation from you.
- I will bless you
- I will make you a blessing.
- I will bless whomever you bless and curse whoever curses you.
- Everyone on Earth will be blessed because of you.[14]

That's it. It's quite a promise. It contains no specifics, so it's remarkable that Abram believes God and obeys. He bundles up his household and his stuff, all the people who are members of his household and their stuff, some extended family and their stuff, and exits. That's a colossal act of faith.

Into this picture enters Sarai, whose husband, at seventy-five, informs her they are embarking on an adventure into the great unknown because God told him to. Based on the information given later in the story,[15] we deduce she is ten years younger than her husband, making her sixty-five

....

[13] God changed Sarai and Abram's names to Sarah and Abraham when he established his covenant with Abraham and promised them a son (Genesis 17:5, 15). So until we reach that point in the story, we'll refer to them as Sarai and Abram.

[14] Genesis 12:1–3.

[15] Genesis 17:17.

years old. So many questions explode in my mind when I think about her situation. Did she wonder if he was developing Alzheimer's and was no longer in complete control of his faculties? Did she question when he had started hearing voices and what should she do about it? Since divorce wasn't a realistic option for a woman back then, did she consider murder? After all, they had no children who might want to know what had happened to Daddy.

Sarai doesn't resort to extreme measures. She accepts her husband's plan, climbs into the caravan's lead wagon with him, and heads into that great unknown. This courageous woman acts upon information she receives second-hand and, consequently, has to trust her husband and the God he trusts. They go "boldly where no man has gone before," long before *Star Trek*. More accurately, where no one they know has gone before, primarily because they have no idea where they're going. Their future is shrouded in mystery.

Eventually, Abram receives a few more particulars of The Plan after he's been unnerved by an escapade that involves rescuing his nephew, Lot.[16] God comes to Abram in a vision and tells him not to be afraid and to keep trusting because there's a great reward in store for him. Abram then points out that he doesn't have any of those offspring things. That makes it rather difficult to arrive at this great reward, and it also means a member of his household will eventually become his heir.

But God is not writing Abram's life story with that ending. He will have a son; God says so. Then God ushers Abram outside to behold the glittering splendour in the night sky and pledges that someday he will have as many descendants as there are stars—too many to even estimate a number. In the crisp air, neck craned to feast on the panorama before him, Abram chooses to believe God again. Because of it, God considers him righteous (in right standing with him).[17]

Sarai's delight must have known no bounds when Abram relayed God's promise about having a son and an unfathomable number of descendants. Unfortunately, she hadn't been able to conceive a child in her youth, and it was important in that culture for a wife to produce babies.

....

[16] Genesis 14.

[17] Genesis 15:4–6.

Hebrew society held the mother's role in high esteem, and Sarai couldn't fulfill that function and responsibility in the family. All her married life, she must have felt inferior to other women who had children, invisible as her peer group shared stories of the amazing things their kids said or did. She would have been like the maiden aunt at family gatherings, whose dreams had included a family but whose reality had unfolded differently, leaving her standing wistfully on the sidelines.

At last, she will have a son—God says so! She may not have baked an End of Infertility cake with "Mommy and Daddy" inscribed on it, but since she and Abram are now rather ancient and still childless, an announcement like that would be stupefying. The adventure of a lifetime is about to begin for them, and Sarai, her husband, and God are all in harmony. This story starts so well.

Ten years later, she still has no son ... or any child. Ten years is a long time to sustain faith in something that probably looks more and more like a faint hope as each year wraps up another unfulfilled chapter in her life. There are no birthday parties or inclusion in the Moms and Tots group at her local community tent. Being classified as a barren woman rather than a mother would have made finding her place in society difficult. But then she is given hope, only to have those hopes dashed on the rocky shores of time. She has left all that was familiar, ventured out into the greater world, and been excited by God's promise of a son, and now that same God appears to have abandoned her. Invisibility has cloaked her for years, but now despair stalks her waking hours.

Waiting for God to act is difficult to endure. When the days turn into months, and the months turn into years, and nothing changes, it's hard to hang on and trust that God is in control and, more importantly, that he cares about us. It wouldn't be nearly so difficult to wait if he gave us a detailed flow chart telling us what he'll do and when, so that we could tick off the milestones as each passes and know which one will be the last. Being a person who thrives on order, that approach would suit me well, but it leaves out one crucial element: faith. God says we need faith to please him.[18] The waiting is all part of building

----

[18] Hebrews 11:6.

that faith and trust, so, like it or not, that's how he works. And he's the one who holds the key to the puzzle. However, if God had given me a specific promise that would change my life when fulfilled, and nothing had happened from one year to the next, the pain of waiting would have become excruciating. That's the lens through which Sarai views life.

And then an epiphany strikes, which is when the whole plan derails. She can fix this! How many of us have concluded that nothing will ever change, that God has forgotten or deserted us, so now it's all up to us? Sarai is standing on that precipice. In her impatience, she decides not to wait for God to execute his promise but to enact her brilliant scheme to engineer God's work for him. Her ingenious solution is to make God's plan come to fruition without God's help. She may not have thought he was incapable of accomplishing what he'd promised, but she was probably tired of waiting, much like any other human might be. How many of us have given up waiting for God to answer a prayer and tried to sort it out ourselves? I'm reasonably sure Sarai is not alone in her impatience.

Her strategy entails having Abram father a child with her Egyptian servant, Hagar.[19] Voilà! Problem solved. Well, not really. Unfortunately, Sarai meddles with God's perfect plan and drags another person into her plot, which has lifelong ramifications for that other person. Volumes could be written on the poor advice women have given their husbands; it goes right back to the first wife, a snake, and some luscious fruit (Adam and Eve), and I'm not exempt from their company. Unfortunately, this was one of those regrettable situations, and Abram decided to comply with his wife's wishes. It doesn't take a doctorate in human psychology to deduce that Sarai's plan was a bad idea from the outset. Still, we benefit from hindsight without the emotional misery she was experiencing clouding our decision-making abilities. From the luxury of my comfy chair and having read the last chapter of the book, it's easy for me to shake my head in wonder at her ill-advised manoeuvring.

Unfortunately for Sarai, life gets worse before it gets better, because although The Surrogate Mother Plan is quite effective, it backfires. Hagar conceives a child and, as a result, becomes contemptuous of her

....

[19] Genesis 16:2.

mistress.[20] There's no joy in the situation for Sarai as Hagar gloats over her new status and treats her mistress as inferior.

If Sarai felt invisible before, I suspect those feelings worsened when the baby arrived, a son named Ishmael. It was a game she had set in motion, one in which she had to live with the aftermath, but she wasn't holding the winning card.

Motherhood is still out of her reach, and now her standing in the family plummets because her husband's focus shifts to this child, and Sarai doesn't have a place in Ishmael's life. Hence, the woman with a dream and a promise lives on the periphery of the family circle with only the echoes of what should have been. Invisible.

Sometimes we feel trapped in our circumstances and think all will be well *when.* Life will be better *when* we have a new job, complete *when* we are married, or happier *when* we lose weight. The list goes on endlessly, and most of us have been there. Sarai learned that life isn't necessarily better *when.* And it's never better when we walk outside the lines God has drawn for us.

These two older people have been waiting for their son for twenty-four long years, and now the last instalment of the promise finally comes.[21] For those twenty-four years, Sarai has tried to find her place in the world. That's an enormous timespan to sustain faith in something that seems increasingly elusive. Feeling invisible during different seasons of life is tough. Still, this season of Sarai's life lasts so long that it has

---

[20] Genesis 16:4.

[21] This is a quick recap of the timeline of the promises God gave Abram and the ages both he and Sarai were at each milestone. Abram was seventy-five years old when God promised he would be the father of a great nation (Genesis 12:1–4). We deduce from Abram's statement in Genesis 17:17 that Sarai was ten years younger, making her sixty-five. When Ishmael was born, Abram was eighty-six years old, making Sarai seventy-six. When Abram was ninety-nine years old, God appeared to him again (Genesis 17:1–14) and made another covenant with him. God changed his name to Abraham and declared that his promise would be fulfilled through the birth of a child to his eighty-nine-year-old wife, Sarai (Genesis 17:21), whom God re-named Sarah (Genesis 17:15). Abraham and Sarah had been waiting for their son for twenty-four years when the last instalment of the promise came. By the time Isaac made his appearance, Abraham was one hundred years old and Sarah was ninety, meaning the entire process took twenty-five years (Harp's Crossing, *Timeline from Abraham to Exodus,* accessed June 16, 2023, https://www.harpscrossing. com/wp-content/uploads/2014/04/Timeline-From-Abram-to-Exodus.pdf).

the hallmarks of Narnia, where it is "always winter, but it never gets to Christmas."[22] Never, that is, until the curse is broken.

Finally, God drops the last pieces of the puzzle into place for Abram, including that they will have a son of their own, Isaac, the following year. God also changes their names to Abraham and Sarah at this time.[23] All around, this is a new beginning for them both, and instead of saying "Oh, good. We'll get right on that," Abraham falls on his face and howls with laughter. It's hysterically funny to him that God decides a good time for them to have a child is when he's one hundred years old and Sarah is ninety.

Where does Sarah fit into this picture? Every time God reveals his plans to Abraham, she's on the sidelines, and her husband relays those plans to her. But when it's time for The Event, the communication route takes a little twist—she learns about it by eavesdropping. Let's see how this part of the chronicle develops.

After God reveals the final covenant, three men appear at Abraham's tent, and they're no ordinary visitors—one is God in human form. Abraham treats them as honoured guests and quickly offers them food and hospitality.

I don't know what Sarah had been doing, but her schedule suddenly changed if she was tackling the laundry or some other domestic chore, or was engrossed in a crossword puzzle to keep her brain from rusting. Her husband comes barrelling into the tent in a frenzy and asks her to make bread posthaste because some guests have arrived. And by the way, one of them is God. Undoubtedly, she sits up and takes notice. It's an "all-hands-on-deck" situation, and Sarah jumps into action while her husband tends to the BBQ. Unexpected company is one thing, but this is not an average tea-and-toast visit. She doesn't even have a stash in her freezer to raid! Ultimately, the meal comes together, and Abraham serves it to the distinguished visitors. Outside under a lovely shade tree, Abraham waits on them as if he has recently graduated from the West Bank Butler Training School.[24]

....

[22] Lewis, *The Lion, the Witch, and the Wardrobe*, 42.

[23] Genesis 17:1–21.

[24] Genesis 18:1–8.

As the guests consume their tea and petit fours, the question comes: *"Where is Sarah your wife?"*[25] She happens to be where all the good wives of her day would have been: in the tent, listening at the door. Well, maybe not all wives would have been listening at the door. Still, when visitors of that import are in her front yard enjoying a dinner party, which she helps prepare extraordinarily quickly for a creaky elder, it isn't surprising that she has her ear to the flap trying to figure out what's going on. The Lord then tells Abraham he will return at about that time the following year, and Abraham and Sarah will be pushing a baby carriage with their son in it.[26] Regardless of the absurdity of their ages, they aren't about to sit back and enjoy retirement. Their child-rearing years are about to commence instead. It sounds like the set-up for a hilarious sitcom.

Sarah's eyes widen, and she may have to stifle her impulse to snort in laughter and disbelief at the preposterous statement she's just over-heard. Imagine, at eighty-nine years old, redecorating the tent to ac-commodate a nursery and maybe finding a nanny the same age as her great-grandchild might have been to help care for the baby. After the unrelenting years of waiting for a child, her reaction now is the same as her husband's. She howls with laughter, only quietly, to herself. Even her menopausal hot flashes are a distant memory, so how, now that she is dried up like a prune, and her husband is equally prunish, are they going to have a wild night of fun and games and create a baby?[27]

Isn't that so like our human nature? Over and over we ask God for something, and then when it doesn't happen the way we expect or when we expect, we almost miss the answer. Our focus is directed so intently in a different direction that we forget that God can do things we can't. But that's why he is God, and we're not.

The delightful dining experience finishes, but there is more happen-ing here than a test of Abraham and Sarah's hospitality and meal-impro-visation skills. God is pursuing Sarah. The heavenly visitor had perceived

---

[25] Genesis 18:9.

[26] Genesis 18:10.

[27] Genesis 18:12.

her inner giggle and speaks to her directly about her reaction before he concludes this extraordinary encounter.[28] She denies it because there's no natural way this person could have known what had happened in her heart and mind, and that knowledge scares her. It's hard to argue with someone with supernatural abilities, and he calls her on it again. This situation is frightening for a mere mortal, one who is about to go where no woman has gone before.

At that moment, I would have felt some trepidation—a lot of trepidation, actually. The thought of having a baby at my age is overwhelming. Picture my husband and me, sprawled on the furniture, almost unconscious, after a day spent with our young grandchildren. The feeling is similar to recovering from the flu, when you feel like every ounce of energy has been sucked from your body ... only there was no flu. Just kids. Now extrapolate that feeling forward another thirty years. There's an abundance of exhaustion in Sarah's future, and this is only the beginning, so it's no wonder the challenge seems daunting.

And then God refocuses the picture for Sarah and Abraham, from what they could not do to what he could. He asks them if anything is too hard for him.[29] Sometimes our view of God is so small we limit what we allow him to do because we can't see past our circumstances and lack of capabilities. Outstanding people exist in every generation who capture a vision of the greatness of God. They walk in tremendous faith, learn to trust God, and ignore or even reject internal and external dissenting opinions trying to lead them astray. And they're willing to pay the price to follow God and not seek their own dreams or desire for security. God challenges both Abraham and Sarah to dare to trust him because nothing is too hard for him. Thus far, they have journeyed by faith, and now the ultimate goal is in sight. God sees them and will use them to show the world his greatness when they have a son in a year.

God honours his promise to Abraham through Sarah, and after twenty-five years of waiting, some of them impatiently, she crosses that divide from invisible to Beloved. More accurately, her perception changes.

....

[28] Genesis 18:13–15.

[29] Genesis 18:14.

God has always loved Sarah and had a master plan in place for her, but now she can see the fulfillment of his promise approaching. He hasn't forgotten this dear lady or cancelled his pledge because she meddled with his plan. Shortcomings and all, God blesses Sarah, and this woman, who has waited for what must seem like forever, becomes pregnant.[30]

For some of the other women in the scriptures we have discussed, their invisibility ends abruptly, and Sarah joins this group. Picture the spectacle of an eighty-nine-year-old woman shopping for maternity wear. Sales associates choke back their giggles when they learn the clothes are for Sarah and not some family member generations younger. Word of a pregnant octogenarian would have gone viral around town, and after all the snickers subsided, chances are people tracked her progress with great interest.

Tabloids and the *Guinness Book of World Records* would love to follow a juicy story like that, but it wasn't fake or a natural anomaly; it was God's power at work. Gone were her days of invisibility because, beautiful though Sarah was, her ninety-year-old face was saggy and wrinkled, and her baby bump screamed young Mama!

In time, this delighted mother gives birth to her child and names him Isaac, as God had instructed.[31] So the adventure begins for this Beloved Daughter.

The Bible doesn't explain the relationship in detail between Sarah and Isaac during his childhood. Yet after years of longing and waiting, I think we can safely assume she fully engaged with every facet of young Isaac's life. Envision her standing by his bed, feasting her eyes on the miracle sleeping there, his chest rhythmically rising and falling, as she thanks God for every breath. I doubt there was a nanny in Isaac's life who took over all of the caregiving duties for the child, although Sarah probably had help. Her aging body showed signs of wear, so assistance may have been necessary. But in my mind, I see her embracing every aspect of child-rearing because God promised her this baby, and it's unlikely she would willingly hand him over to someone else's charge.

....

[30] Genesis 21:1–2a.

[31] Genesis 17:19.

Sarah is zealously devoted to Isaac and loves him fiercely. She watches over and protects him, not allowing anyone to displace him or threaten his inheritance. For that reason, she ultimately expels Ishmael and Hagar from their home.[32] The next chapter will explore Hagar's role in this saga and her parallel journey.

Sarah lives to be 127 years of age,[33] meaning Isaac was about 37 years old at the time of her death. Well into his adult years, she can enjoy her miracle son. God doesn't just use her as a baby incubator and say, "Thanks, Sarah. You're finished now. Come home to heaven, and we'll take it from here." He allows her to raise her child and enjoy him for many years; he sees the desire of her heart.

Although the biblical account's primary focus is to note the history of Abraham's line through Isaac, Sarah is a critical player. She is not invisible. She's a Beloved Daughter entrusted with raising this heir who makes a mark on history and will to the end of time. Parenting is of crucial significance. Isaac doesn't magically develop the character traits and skills he needs to become a man of consequence whom God can use. If Sarah hadn't poured into his life and instilled the discipline and values she did, Isaac might have become a tragic "could have been" cast along the wayside of life. She plays a fundamental role in moulding him in his formative years, shaping the framework for the man he becomes.

The love between mother and son is not a one-way street. Although we don't have colourful specifics to fill in the details of their relationship, we know there's a lasting connection between their heartstrings. Isaac and his wife, Rebekah, consummate their marriage in his mother's tent.[34] If their relationship had been contentious, I don't think Isaac would have used that venue for his wedding night but would have found a place where Sarah's shadow wasn't hanging over him. When his mother dies, his new wife comforts and helps her husband through his grief.[35] That speaks to me of the depth of love mother and son share, and to

---

[32] Genesis 21:8–14.

[33] Genesis 23:1–2.

[34] Genesis 24:67.

[35] Genesis 24:67.

the end, the ties between them are strong. Not only is Sarah a Beloved Daughter of the Most High God, but she is also a beloved mother.

Sarah was a flawed woman who blundered spectacularly with the whole surrogate mother disaster, but she finished well—no longer invisible but as a Beloved Daughter. If ever you feel you have ruined everything because of a poor decision, and you think God can't use you as a result, take heart, my friend. Sarah was not a perfect specimen of womanhood, but do you know where she eventually landed? In the Hall of Faith. Hebrews 11 is often called that because it contains Old Testament heroes, both men and women, whom God commended for their extraordinary faith. Reading that chapter is like walking down a long hallway with paintings of outstanding people lining the walls. People who, despite their circumstances, chose to trust God and not their own understanding. People whom God asked to do outrageous things, like Noah, who built an ark because a flood was coming. Noah had no concept of an ark or flood, but he trusted God and accomplished his mission. In that auspicious lineup, along that hallway, we find Sarah. Not only is she listed with this remarkable group, but she's the first woman mentioned.

Hebrews 11:11 says, "*By faith Sarah herself received power to conceive, even when she was past the age, <u>since she considered him faithful who had promised</u>*" (emphasis added). Her picture isn't in that gallery because she was Abraham's wife, an appendage of her husband. She's there because she believed God, a woman of faith in her own right. The promise given to Abraham—that he would be the father of many nations, and Sarah would be the mother of their son—would never have come to fruition had she not believed that her dried-up bits could conceive and carry a child. And now she is commemorated in the Hall of Faith, where only people of exceptional faith reside and where she's linked forever with those estimable men and women. What an inspiring Beloved Daughter!

The woman who struggled to find her place and was dried up like a prune and invisible for years did not remain on the sidelines forever. Her story gives me tremendous hope. God is there even when we feel we are floundering alone, like Sarah. And he still loves and cares for us and can use us to accomplish his purposes, even when we've done idiotic things. Who knows what God can do with those of us, also mere mortals, who follow Sarah's lead and trust God because "*he is faithful who promised*"? That path is sometimes frightening because we have no idea where we're going, but taking the plunge and bravely surrendering control allows us to follow the one who promised. After all, just like Sarah, we are Beloved Daughters of the same God who sees us too.

3

From Outcast to Beloved —Hagar

Before there was the *Hagar the Horrible* comic strip featuring the beloved red-bearded Viking in his horned helmet, the Bible tells us of a woman with the same name. The biblical Hagar was anything but a comic figure. Her tale is the flip side of the story Sarah set in motion and contains little to spark laughter. But the same God who loved Sarah pursued and compassionately revealed himself to Hagar when she was alone and feeling invisible. This servant girl endured great hardship, including being expelled from her home, and although some of the problems were of her own making, God didn't abandon her. This headstrong young woman was not unseen or ignored by a God who couldn't be bothered with her. She was his Beloved Daughter.

Join me as we learn more about a God who sees his hidden daughters and who loves us regardless of the reason for our circumstances.

Hagar triggers conflicting emotions in me. Sympathy tugs at my heart-strings, but at the same time, my parental viewpoint kicks in. I wonder why she didn't consider the consequences of her disdainful attitude and resulting behaviour and realize she was setting herself up for trouble. But then I look at my own life and know that I too have made choices and behaved in ways that couldn't possibly have ended well, yet I per-sisted in them. Some of us learn through experience—translation: we don't necessarily make the wisest choice at the outset. However, with maturity, many of us realize the value of forethought before we charge down a path we will later regret, or react in a way that will only bring remorse. Unfortunately, even age doesn't guarantee we will always select the advisable option. Proverbs 8:35–36a says, "*For whoever finds* [wisdom] *finds life and obtains favour from the Lord, but he who fails to find* [wisdom] *injures himself.*" If only we heeded that warning. But we, like Hagar and Sarah too, sometimes learn the hard way. The really hard way.

So how did Hagar wind up in a predicament? Well, it wasn't entirely her own doing. As mentioned in the previous chapter, since it appeared that Abram and Sarai were nearing their expiry dates with no hint of a baby in sight, Sarai devised an ingenious solution to the problem. Since God didn't seem to honour his promise of a child, she assumed responsibility for family planning and conscripted her household servant as a surrogate mother. Which is where it all went wrong—terribly wrong. Especially for Hagar. The previous chapter contains a fuller description of the promise given to Abram and Sarai, so if you haven't read that chapter yet, you might want to do so first and then return to this one.

As a servant, Hagar didn't hold a position of power in her relationship with her mistress. Her thoughts on the advisability of Sarai's idea were irrelevant because of her low social standing and place in the household. The role of a servant was to serve, not to question the master's actions and decisions. So it was in Hagar's best interest to be seen when necessary and not heard for life to run smoothly. Very little in her world was under her control. Hagar was the invisible woman who did the grunt work, any task her mistress assigned, and her feelings about those duties didn't concern anyone.

Thus, in compliance with Sarai's wish, Abram cozied up with Hagar, who conceived a child,[36] and the whole dynamic and balance of power in the home shifted. Today we would refer to that as unintended consequences. Hagar was pregnant, her mistress was not, and she revelled in her new position of power, behaving as though she had all the rights and privileges belonging to the lady of the manor. As a result, she became arrogant and contemptuous of the woman who held that role.[37]

Reading that scenario makes me cringe because I know that an attitude like that can't possibly lead anywhere good—my parental point of view kicking in again. When I was a child, my mother wouldn't stand for any gloating from my siblings or me when good fortune befell one of us, and I tried to raise my children with that same value. Unfortunately, Hagar missed that lesson. Admittedly, hers was not an unusual human reaction, but she ultimately paid a dear price for her moment of glory. Let's pick up the story there.

Sarai is livid because she isn't going to stand for a servant despising her, someone who has been placed in a position of honour only to abuse the privilege. When her plans don't work out as expected, Sarai does what many of us do in similar circumstances: she blames someone else. Sadly for Abram, he's the target. Sarai launches into a tirade worthy of a political pundit on YouTube, claiming the whole debacle is his fault.[38] Poor Abram. There he is, caught between two warring women, when sleeping with Hagar wasn't even his idea in the first place. And for his trouble, he gets blamed when everything goes awry. Since he's embroiled in this fiasco with no easy way out, he responds by refusing to be drawn into the fray, saying, "She is your servant, do whatever you want."[39] Not good, at least not for Hagar. She has picked the wrong person to antagonize, because it's a fight she can't possibly win. This lamentable drama is a no-win situation for all the cast members.

....

[36] Genesis 16:3.

[37] Genesis 16:4.

[38] Genesis 16:5.

[39] Genesis 16:6 (paraphrase).

And then the whole scheme begins to unravel. The plan for the promised son, God's plan, turns into a home filled with discord and strife, because that's what happens when we try to manipulate situations ourselves and don't allow God to work in his time and his way. The result is that Sarai treats Hagar "harshly,"[40] and we can be sure she doesn't invite her to a tea party to discuss poetry. Since Hagar is a servant and not a wife, nasty duties and long hours likely result from her impudent behaviour, even though the offender is pregnant. The message that she is nothing more than a despicable gnat in the household is undoubtedly relayed loudly and clearly by her mistress. Not good for Hagar at all.

Unsurprisingly, Hagar snaps and decides the great unknown is a better place to live than the great known with Sarai, so she runs away.[41] To some degree, she brings her predicament upon herself; however, she's still a young woman, alone, with nowhere to turn. Invisible. No friends to whom she can choke out her tale of woe. No grandmotherly figure to offer her hope and wisdom or dispense some tough love, then hug her until the storm passes and her weeping ends. Hagar is alone, completely and utterly alone.

Have you ever felt that way? A situation you may have had a hand in creating, or not, that turned out poorly, but in the end you felt as if you had no one to help carry the unbearable load? I have. It's not a pleasant place to live. Many years ago, our church went through an enormous upheaval, and many of the congregation decided to part ways and attend elsewhere. At the time, I had a toddler, was pregnant with our second child, and was in charge of Sunday school. Seemingly weekly, someone called to inform me they had decided to worship elsewhere and would no longer teach a class, leaving me with positions to fill and no one to meet the need. My husband and I chose to stay with the church, and we watched most of our close friends leave. It was an emotionally upsetting and confusing time for everyone, and I'm sure my being pregnant didn't help my emotional state. Aside from my husband, who was experiencing the same loss, I felt I had nowhere to turn for support

---

[40] Genesis 16:6.

[41] Genesis 16:6.

and encouragement. Invisible. Not having family in the area, when my baby was born, I didn't have the support system and friendships that surrounded me with our first child. I have never felt so alone.

Over the years, the Lord has restored many of those friendships, and the rifts between church members have healed. Although some became part of other congregations, the relationships have mended, and we are truly grateful. Was it a horrible experience I would never wish on anyone? Yes. Was God faithful through it all? Yes, again.

Hagar is about to discover the reality of God's faithfulness herself.

Having fled her home, she has no money to check into the Desert Springs Resort in the wilderness, so she stops near a spring.[42] There sits poor Hagar—hot, pregnant, uncomfortable, discouraged, and likely wondering what to do. Having given little or no thought to her plan, she's probably also starving. Her problems don't appear to matter to anyone, and not being able to solve them herself, she is distraught and demoralized.

My heart breaks for that young woman in such a desperate situation. God seems to wait until we have no other recourse—when no matter how hard we try, we can't manoeuvre our way out of a dilemma ourselves—before he steps in. And so it was with Hagar.

In deep anguish, utterly invisible to the world, Hagar sees an angel approach her.[43] I have not knowingly spoken with any angels recently, but I'd be stunned if an angel appeared at the moment of my greatest need. God pursues Hagar to that lonely place and sends an angel to help. Think about that with me for a moment. God doesn't send a delivery person with a pizza for her dining pleasure. He sends an angel, and angels come from heaven. God sends a messenger from heaven to help her when no other options are available in a dusty, dry, lonely desert. In my books, that's personal ministration on a level so far beyond my conception that I would need binoculars even to look for it on the horizon. Hagar feels invisible and unloved by everyone in her world, yet God reaches out to her in love.

[42] Genesis 16:7.

[43] Genesis 16:7.

The angel asks her, "... *where have you come from and where are you going?*"[44] Hagar responds only to the first part of the query, possibly because she doesn't have an answer to the second. Rather than skirting the issue, she openly confesses she is running away from her mistress. The refrain from the children's book *The Gingerbread Man* comes to my mind here because I've read it so many times, first to my children and now to my grandchildren, "I have run away from an old man, and an old woman, and I can run away from you too!"[45] Hagar had run away from an old woman and an old man, but she didn't run away from the angel. A haughty attitude lands her in this predicament, but she takes full responsibility for her actions and doesn't hedge or justify her behaviour. This distressed soul doesn't even do what many of us do or what Sarai had previously done with Abram—that is, blame someone else. She behaves like an adult and states briefly that she has run away.[46] Since her physical and emotional energy are exhausted, there's no benefit in hiding the truth. Hagar lays out her situation, no more, no less.

The love God extends to her through the angel is not likely in the form Hagar sought. He doesn't begin with warm fuzzies and assure her that he will fix everything. We often ask God to solve a problem for us, but unfortunately, that doesn't seem to be the way he usually operates. The angel flatly tells her she needs to return to her mistress, and not just go back with a surly attitude and stomp around the kitchen, slamming pots. She is to *submit* to Sarai.[47]

Have you ever noticed that when God steps in to rescue us, he asks us to do things we don't want to do? Such as offering two different options, but neither is desirable? He's very good at putting us in situations where we must humble ourselves, swallow our pride, and make things right. Canadians are known worldwide for our constant apologies, like when we accidentally jostle someone while shopping and our immediate response is, "Sorry!" Canadian or not, that's vastly different from having

---

[44] Genesis 16:8.

[45] Schmidt, *The Gingerbread Man,* 13.

[46] Genesis 16:8.

[47] Genesis 16:9.

to go to someone and give a heartfelt apology for something we've done. The first is easy, an automatic response programmed into us since childhood; the second can be challenging and requires a dedicated effort to humble our pride to do it.

Thinking I was being helpful, I once inadvertently offended a store sales associate. Unfortunately, what resulted was the opposite of what I'd intended. However, it wasn't the time to try and remedy the situation, so I had to return a few days later to apologize. That wasn't an easy conversation to initiate, and the need to have it weighed heavily on me until I could go back and ask for forgiveness. We are so invested in our pride that even as I write about this memory, I wonder if I can relate a different illustration that shows me in a more positive light—or better yet, one from someone else's life! Pride dies a bitter death even in a discussion on humility. Humbling ourselves doesn't come easily to any of us. But God hates pride, and over and over he calls us to take that step of our own volition and humble ourselves. He wanted submission from Hagar, and the genesis of that submission was humility.

In James 4:6b–7a, we're told, "*God opposes the proud but gives grace to the humble. Submit yourselves therefore to God.*" This statement doesn't include a conditional stipulation: "If you feel like it." Many times I'd like that proviso included because I'd like to take the easy way out. But somehow he doesn't see it that way. These verses show that pride blocks the grace God wants to offer us, and what's more, he "*opposes the proud.*"[48]

The Canadian Oxford Dictionary defines "submit" as "consent to … abide by a certain condition or limitation etc.; surrender (oneself) to."[49] Submitting is not a natural human inclination, and even Jesus, centuries later, struggled with complete surrender in Gethsemane. He prayed concerning his coming death, "*Father, if you are willing, remove this cup from me. Nevertheless, not my will, but yours, be done.*"[50] Hagar is—we all are—in good company as we navigate the challenges of growth.

....

[48] James 4:6.

[49] The Canadian Oxford Dictionary, 2nd ed., s.v. "Submit, v."

[50] Luke 22:42.

Let's return to Hagar and see how her situation unfolds.

The angel tells the runaway to return home and yield to Sarai's authority. In obeying that instruction, she will be submitting to God. But that isn't the end of the story. The angel doesn't just say, "Go home and behave yourself," but gives her hope in what she perceives as a hopeless situation. He tells her she will have so many offspring it will be impossible to count them.[51] The angel certainly doesn't mean Hagar will spend the rest of her life pregnant, which I don't think would have brought her hope, but she will have innumerable descendants.

He then informs her that the child she is carrying is a son and instructs her to name him Ishmael *"because the Lord has listened to your affliction."*[52] That touches the wounded place deep in her heart, where she's suffering tremendous emotional pain. God listens and doesn't berate her for her part in the drama in which she finds herself, or read a list of wrongs she has committed. Doesn't that amaze you? Sometimes we fear taking our problems and worries to God because we think he'll judge us rather than help us, or that what we've done is so appalling he'll turn his back on us. In Hagar's state, I don't think it's likely that she did a happy dance as the reality of that statement resonated with her. Still, quite possibly, tears ran down her face as she recognized the truth: she wasn't forgotten and alone but had just moved from invisible to Beloved Daughter.

That's the good news; now, the bad news. The angel gives her some general details about her baby and who he will become. That revelation may have fallen into the TMI (Too Much Information) category from her point of view. He will be a wild character, antagonistic and hostile to the world, and that same hostility will be returned to him.[53] I'm not sure hearing, "It's a boy! Oh, and by the way, he'll hate everyone in the world, and they will hate him," would reassure a pregnant girl. It's a good news/bad news scenario, but God hears her in her distress, and she will have that knowledge to cherish and cling to when her son becomes

---

[51] Genesis 16:10.

[52] Genesis 16:11b.

[53] Genesis 16:12.

a challenge. Her response is, "*You are a God of seeing … Truly here I have seen him who looks after me.*"[54] Hagar belongs to a Father who genuinely cares about what happens in her life. But there is trouble ahead.

Ultimately, Abraham and Sarah (their new names) conceive and bear a son named Isaac. When Sarah has weaned Isaac, Abraham throws a huge party to commemorate that important milestone in his miracle son's life, but Sarah's day has an unpleasant wrinkle. In the middle of the revelry, she glances over and notices Ishmael, Hagar's son, laughing, and the implication is that it's a mocking laugh.[55] With that one glimpse, the joy drains from every pore of her body, and her delightful day is in ruins.

As a result of that arrogance and disdain on Ishmael's part, Sarah orders Abraham, in no uncertain terms, to banish Hagar and her son from their home and their lives.[56] Ishmael isn't going to be an heir with her son if she has anything to do with it. Ishmael is in trouble this time, and his mother gets dragged into it along with him. The biblical account tells us that Abraham isn't happy about evicting them because Ishmael is his son. However, God intervenes and instructs Abraham to comply with whatever Sarah tells him to do—God actually says that![57] He reassures Abraham and affirms that he will create a nation through Ishmael because this boy too is Abraham's son. The proviso is that Abraham's line, his name, will be carried through Isaac, not Ishmael.

Now behold one of the most forlorn verses I think I've ever read in the Bible. Genesis 21:14 says:

> So Abraham rose early in the morning and took bread and a skin of water and gave it to Hagar, putting it on her shoulder, along with the child, and sent her away. And she departed and wandered in the wilderness of Beersheba.

---

[54] Genesis 16:13.

[55] Genesis 21:9.

[56] Genesis 21:10.

[57] Genesis 21:12.

Reading that verse, I feel utter despair for poor Hagar. There she is, with a small child on her shoulders, given only what food and water she can carry, and essentially told, "See you, have a good life." So she again finds herself wandering in the wilderness, despondent and invisible. Only this time she doesn't have a home to which she can return, and she has a young child in tow. Two mouths to feed, no food or water left, parched, hungry, and dejected—things do not look good. Her state of affairs bears a striking resemblance to the picture of Hell described in Dante's *The Divine Comedy*, "Through me you pass into the city of woe: Through me you pass into eternal pain ... All hope abandon, ye who enter here."[58]

With no alternatives left, the outcast places her precious boy under some bushes and removes herself from his immediate vicinity. Hagar settles far enough away to avoid watching, in vivid detail, her beloved son suffer a miserable, horrible, really bad death. And then, having exhausted all the tools in her arsenal, she weeps.[59] Her heartbroken sobs pierce the vast emptiness where this distraught mother sits as despair envelops and threatens to smother her. In identical circumstances, I would be amazed if I lasted as long as she did before abandoning hope.

What an awful image. If ever there was a word picture that epitomizes loneliness and dejection, this is it. At times in my life, I've felt invisible and not enjoyed it, but this takes invisibility to another level. Hagar was rejected like trash to fend for herself and her child, and not a soul in the world cared—this world. However, there's another realm where someone did care. And again, God pursued her. Genesis 21:17–18 rolls back the curtain and reveals what happened in the heavenly realm:

> And God heard the voice of the boy, and the angel of God called to Hagar from heaven and said to her, "What troubles you, Hagar? Fear not, for God has heard the voice of the boy where he is. Up! Lift up the boy, and hold him fast with your hand, for I will make him into a great nation."

---

[58] Alighieri, *The Divine Comedy*, Canto III, 1, 2, 9.

[59] Genesis 21:15–16.

God hears Hagar's son, and an angel speaks directly to her from heaven. God hasn't forgotten about this overwrought mother or her son. Just think what that experience would have been like, sitting in the wilderness, sobbing because your physical and emotional resources are gone, and a voice speaks to you from heaven and says God hears your son. Her heavenly Father isn't missing in action. Notice that the angel asks about her feelings, "*What troubles you, Hagar?*"[60] He doesn't jump in and immediately start pontificating about great things that will happen. He acknowledges her distress and, in so doing, validates her feelings, and only afterwards begins to shine a light on a brighter future. Hagar is important to God, and not just for her part in the bigger picture.

Hope in a hopeless situation is what she needs, and the angel offers it to her. Ishmael will live—not just survive—to the end of his natural lifespan, and God will make him the patriarch of a vast nation. The angel also instructs Hagar regarding her role in fulfilling that prophecy. She's to get up, retrieve her son, and tightly hold his hand. God has given her the responsibility of raising this little person, so she has to summon her courage, start moving, and guide her difficult child into adulthood. The kernel of a whole nation lies in him, and God entrusted Hagar with helping to bring that future nation to fruition. That sounds like a daunting undertaking, but God knows she is a strong lady, and given the right way to channel that strength, and with his help, she can accomplish it. Hagar is no longer invisible, a player in someone else's Game of Life; she is a Beloved Daughter, someone seen by God and with an enormous responsibility to fulfill.

Do you know what happens next? God opens Hagar's eyes and she sees a well nearby.[61] We don't know if her distress initially blinds her to its existence or if God created a new well for her. Possibly he had deliberately prevented her from seeing it so she would come to him for deliverance. Whatever the reason, God enables her to notice the life-giving water she and her son so desperately need, and she races over and fills her water bottle. That would have been the most refreshing

---

[60] Genesis 21:17.

[61] Genesis 21:19.

drink of her little boy's life! As she quenches her own burning thirst, I'm convinced she knows God is and will continue to be the source of her life and sustenance.

Hagar and her son then make a new life in the wilderness. There's a strong possibility that this mother had prematurely gray hair from raising her boy, but she held his hand, and Genesis 21:20a says, *"And God was with the boy, and he grew up."* He probably needed stitches periodically along the way and may have had a broken bone or two. Since Hagar and Ishmael both had forceful personalities, it likely wasn't easy for mother or son, but *"God was with the boy."* The good news is, Hagar wasn't invisible, abandoned to navigate the world of childrearing alone. God was actively involved in her son's life.

Ishmael became an expert at shooting things with a bow and arrow and enjoyed the life of a boy living in a wild place.[62] Eventually he married an Egyptian woman—chosen by his mother, nonetheless![63]— and ultimately became the patriarch of an immense nation.

The story of Hagar and Ishmael is fraught with many difficulties, but even though it's complicated and challenging, we see a God who loves and pursues an invisible woman through it all. He rescues her more than once, but not by solving all her problems. Instead, he corrects her when she needs to act like an adult and no one else is around to direct her toward responsible decisions. Best of all, though, he pursues this lonely outcast in her darkest moments and times of greatest need. He sees her. So even though she's banished from home and hidden in the wilderness, she is not invisible to him.

God doesn't select an impeccable specimen of humanity to whom to minister. Despite her deficiencies, he chooses to love an immature, headstrong, and flawed person. Being human, we don't always make

....

[62] Genesis 21:20–21.

[63] Genesis 21:21.

wise choices, but God loves and cares for us even if we've made a mess of things. The Bible says in 1 John 1:9, *"If we confess our sins, he is faithful and just to forgive us our sins and to cleanse us from all unrighteousness."*

Hagar travelled a long and arduous route from an invisible outcast to a Beloved Daughter, and many of us wander along bumpy paths too. But don't discount the value of the difficulties. The pithy observation by the American industrialist Henry J. Kaiser applies well to the hard parts of life: "Problems are only opportunities in work clothes."[64] If Hagar had remained in quiet servitude her entire life, she never would have experienced the delight of knowing the depth of God's love for her. Yes, she created some of her own difficulties, and sometimes you and I do the same. But God was with her on each step of her journey, and he will be for us too. His eyes are on each one of us. So put on your work clothes, carry on, and keep trusting, Beloved Daughter.

---

[64] Kaiser, *United States Congressional Record—Senate,* August 25, 1967, 24155, para. 1.

4

From Naughty Girl to Beloved
—Rahab

I nvisibility isn't always a state thrust upon us; sometimes we quietly choose it. Many of us live with the poor decisions we made earlier in life or their consequences. Eventually, we may feel that history and our shame prevent us from impacting our world for God because we're not exemplary enough to accomplish great things. Invisibility is a shroud under which we function within a limited realm and where others expect little from us.

Breaking the barriers of invisibility and shame takes courage, but on the other side of that wall is the rewarding life of the Beloved Daughter. Let's look together at a naughty girl named Rahab who became a Beloved Daughter despite her less-than-stellar past. Not only was she lauded in scripture for her outstanding faith and took her place in the Hall of Faith in Hebrews 11, but she also became an ancestor of Jesus. Explore how God pursued and used someone who refused to remain invisible and accept the lie that she couldn't do something great for him because she wasn't good enough.

This tale begins as many do, long ago and in a place far away, but the dark and stormy night part may be debatable. Joshua, the leader of the Israelite people, sends two spies to scope out the land God promised them, specifically the city of Jericho.[65] I imagine these men need a low profile to carry out their undercover operation, so they don't check into the Israeli Embassy in Jericho. They seek accommodation where the locals won't likely pay much attention to their comings and goings. They land at the house of an unsuspecting prostitute named Rahab, which Bible scholars widely believe was an inn.[66] Already we see God at work pursuing Rahab, because they could have chosen any local Bed and Breakfast with an enticing menu, or sheets that feel like butter, tucked away in a peaceful neighbourhood.

Quietly minding her own business, Rahab welcomes her visitors to her establishment. They don't greet her with, "Hi. Nice place you have here. We've come to check out your city and see how hard it will be to take it from you." As the narrative unfolds, it becomes increasingly clear that Rahab is a perceptive lady. Her antennae are on alert, and she knows these are not your average travellers just stopping to rest for the night and to catch some Netflix. She quickly deduces they are from Israel and are no ordinary visitors.

As it turns out, someone figures out why her guests are there and reports their presence and business to the King of Jericho.[67] Since the job of spies is covert, invisibility is a good thing for them, but their assignment becomes tricky when their secret deployment is no longer a secret.

The king sends a message to Rahab and orders her to bring out the men staying there because their activities will not be advantageous to the town.[68] *Really* not advantageous, since their mission, which they chose

[65] Joshua 2:1a.

[66] Joshua 2:1b.

[67] Joshua 2:2.

[68] Joshua 2:3.

to accept, is to report back to their leader, a potential conqueror. That doesn't bode well for the monarchy's future, and the king doesn't plan to invite them to the palace for drinks and a quiet evening of board games.

There is Rahab, an average prostitute and innkeeper, suddenly thrust into the middle of a rapidly unfolding drama. Because of her occupation, she probably holds a low social position and is likely accustomed to being invisible beyond her immediate realm. However, she is so much more than the designation on her tax form or the neon sign flashing above her door: Prostitute.

Due to our preconceived and stereotypical notions about what that label indicates, we may judge her character. And we might be wrong on many counts. All humans are more than what we do. In my crisis, the one that brought me to this study, the cry deep within my heart was that I wanted people to see me for who I am and not just for what I do, even though they are intertwined. So often we see people through the lens of actions and labels and miss the heart underneath that drives them. Behaviours and activities can become default settings, surfacing as if on autopilot, or are deliberate barriers we erect to keep others from peeking behind the curtain.

Think of the waitress bustling about serving breakfast, with whom you exchange general pleasantries and whom you think of as just someone filling a role. In reality, she may be a single mom struggling to make ends meet, dreaming of someday becoming a social worker, owning a restaurant, or becoming a librarian. You see a waitress, but she is so much more. Or we judge a person by her actions because she doesn't fit in our box of what we consider acceptable. Thus, we dismiss her and refuse to look deeper, beyond the obvious, and glimpse her essence.

At first glance, we may relegate Rahab to that second category. Looking closer, we realize that this seemingly insignificant business operator is not someone we should disregard because of her occupation, or assume is a compliant little lady who robotically follows orders when men with power try to push her around. This intelligent woman thinks for herself and quickly and accurately assesses the situation rather than accepting the official position without question. Rahab is a creative problem solver with a few clever ideas ready to employ if needed.

How do you think this lady who dwells in the shadows felt when she received a direct message from the king? Intimidated? Frightened of possible repercussions if she didn't comply? Was she upset because she provided lodging for travellers, minded her own business, and suddenly the king expected her to hand them over to the men looming at her door? Rahab had a vested interest in Jericho because she earned her livelihood there, but this shrewd lady also knew why her guests planned to sneak around the city.

Now she's ensnared in a volatile situation that may not end well for her or her visitors. When the emissaries from the king arrive at her door and insist upon seeing her guests, she looks at them in all innocence and tells them a blatant lie. My paraphrase reads, "Oh, I'm so sorry, you just missed them. Yes, they were here, but I had no idea where they were from. Just as the gate was about to close for the night, they left the city. I have absolutely no clue where they went, but if you hurry, you may be able to catch them."[69]

The truth was that Rahab had foreseen this eventuality, taken the spies to her roof, and hidden them. They aren't lounging at a bistro table, enjoying the view while drinking lemonade until the threat passed. They're lying under stalks of flax she's drying in the sun, probably trying not to sneeze and reveal their position.[70] The whole incident is an example of craftiness at its best. Having accepted her explanation, the king's men race out of the city in hot pursuit, and the gates clang shut behind them.[71] The closed gates will trap the spies inside if they're still hiding in the city, blocking any escape.

The good news is that God was in complete control of the entire situation. As we look at this story from the perspective provided by time and distance, it seems simple to discern God's hand orchestrating the events on behalf of both the scouts and Rahab. In life, we don't acquire that perspective until later when the turmoil subsides and the episode is neatly tucked into our backpack of experience. But in the present

[69] Joshua 2:4–5.

[70] Joshua 2:6.

[71] Joshua 2:7.

moment is where faith fits into the picture. I prefer when billboards line the road, spelling out directions and encouragement to help me limp along. However, faith and trust are essential in those places of uncertainty, especially when it seems as if everything supporting us has disappeared. We may feel isolated from the rest of the world, but that's when the Father draws close and reaches out to his Beloved Daughters.

In Rahab's world, espionage isn't a field in which she has much experience. I don't see her donning dark glasses and a trench coat, skulking around corners and dim alleys, trying to assess the enemy's threat level. However, she's willing to take a huge personal risk for one reason. She has faith. What sparks that faith in a woman who is invisible to the world at large, who fills a seemingly minute role in the grand scheme of things, and who isn't even a woman of impeccable credentials?

Whispers are circulating in her community, and she has heard things. Before tucking her visitors under their temporary blanket of flax stalks on their rooftop hideaway, their host informs them that she knows who they are. She opens this discussion with the bold statement, "*I know that the Lord has given you the land, and that the fear of you has fallen upon us …*"[72] What a statement! Rahab is not an atheist. This woman knows the Lord is the initiating cause behind the astounding occurrences in the world around her. Shrewdly, she deduces two points of great import, which she relays to her resident spies. The first is that she knows she's living in a doomed place. If you're aware that the Lord has given your homeland to someone else, your future there is probably not rosy, and your continued existence may not look too promising either. Her second observation is that everyone in her city is terrified and hopeless due to the rumours circulating. The buzz in the town about the Israelites' feats, such as crossing the Red Sea when they left Egypt en masse, has reached her ears.[73]

Can you imagine how that would make you feel, hearing that the sea had supernaturally parted and an enormous throng of people had walked across on dry land?[74] A phenomenon of that magnitude would

---

[72] Joshua 2:9a.

[73] Joshua 2:10.

[74] Exodus 14.

be tough to ignore. Not only was it a miraculous event in itself, but now there was a swarm of homeless people traipsing—somewhere. That would have been ominous for Rahab, with good reason, and I'm sure she'd discussed it at length with her neighbours.

Additionally, Jericho's occupants had heard the frightening tale about how the King of Sihon of the Amorites had foolishly refused the horde of peaceful wanderers safe passage through his territory.[75] To add to his folly, he sent his people to attack them in the wilderness—bad move. The Israelites defeated him, took his land, and moved in. Previously, he had conquered and occupied the land belonging to the King of Moab, so they now possessed that too. They only planned to amble on through, but King Sihon unwisely picked a fight with them.[76] It was foolish enough to refuse to cooperate with God, but to start a war with his people was madness on an epic scale.

The Israelites were a force to contend with, so it was no wonder Jericho's residents were faint-hearted when reports of spies from this formidable foe surfaced in their midst. Rahab knew what was ahead; she'd heard it all before. Her city was in the crosshairs of the Israelites, and she knew how the story would end.

How do you think she felt with impending doom hanging over her like an anvil? Was she nervously waiting for a trumpet blast in the distance and the chilling sound of clanging spears and boots thundering toward her home? Did she feel alone and hopeless, invisible? Rahab could have chosen to sneak a message to the king and then stand by innocently as the men were apprehended and hauled away.

Interestingly, she chooses to ally herself with the enemy. That very enemy is now hiding on her roof, and she's the one who concealed them there. That's quite a clear case of collusion, and she has crossed a line of no return.

There's a reason for her actions beyond pure self-preservation. Listen to what she says to her visitors: "*And as soon as we heard it* [tales of the Israelites' unfolding exploits], *our hearts melted, and there was no spirit left*

....

[75] Joshua 2:10.

[76] Numbers 21:21–26.

in any man because of you, for the Lord your God, he is God in the heavens above and on the earth beneath."[77] The Israelite conquest is something Rahab and the people of Jericho have never before encountered, and she perceives something unusual in the situation. She knows this army isn't trouncing all in their wake using their natural abilities. God, the one and only true God, is making a place in the world for his people. So this courageous woman exercises faith, takes a stand, and allies herself with the true God. And this is the moment she crosses the great divide from invisible woman to Beloved Daughter.

God works outside the box of our accepted norms and practices, and too often we forget he can do so. But we create those boxes, not him. Thankfully, he doesn't forget he can work around our rules and regimens and draws people to himself in places and ways we tend to discount. And that is what he does with Rahab. This woman catches a glimpse of the greatness of the God of the Israelites. She puts her faith and trust in that God, and he makes a way for her.

And now, since Rahab has helped the spies, it's their turn to help her. Not content to settle for any scraps that may fall her way, this woman of faith has a clear idea of what she wants, uses her voice, and strikes a bargain with the spies. She's not willing to retreat into the background once again, invisible. Life and death are at stake, and the deal is too important to let the secret agents hold the position of power in the negotiations. The agreement Rahab reaches isn't to merely save her own life but to rescue her entire clan, her *"father, mother, brothers, sisters, and all who belong to them"* with her.[78] The spies readily accept her terms because she has been kind to them. During the pandemonium about to descend on their city, this Beloved Daughter knows God will care for her and her loved ones. It isn't a faint hope or a wish; she knows it's a reality before it happens. No wonder she's commended later in scripture for her faith.[79]

Negotiations complete, Rahab helps the men escape. She ties a bright red rope in her window and, using all her strength as the cord

----

[77] Joshua 2:11 (emphasis added).

[78] Joshua 2:13–14.

[79] Hebrews 11:31.

cuts into her hands, braces herself. One by one, she carefully lowers each man over the city wall on which her house stands. They thump to safety below, and as she holds her raw and bleeding hands, she further instructs them to run for the hills and stay there for three days until their pursuers return home. Then, when all is clear, they can return to their encampment.[80] She has carefully considered this course of action and doesn't just tell the men, "They're gone, run!" The sequence of events ahead is predictable. She knows how the scenario will unfold: where the authorities are most likely to search and where they are not (due mainly to her misdirection), and how long they will dedicate to the hunt before admitting defeat.

Before the undercover operatives accept that lifeline out of the city, they establish clearly defined conditions to honour the deal. It's only binding if, when they enter to conquer the city, Rahab has tied the same scarlet cord in the same window through which they now escape. Furthermore, every member of her family she wishes to protect must be waiting with her, ready to leave. If any of them exit the house and enter the street, their fate will be in their own hands. Conversely, if they're in the designated place and something happens to them, the Israelites will be held responsible. These are not frivolous terms but are of grave importance. The final stipulation maintains that the entire contract will be null and void if anyone dares to breathe a word of their pact.[81] Rahab isn't just a pretty face but also an excellent negotiator. Not someone easily put into a box of any shape.

After three days and the immediate danger has passed, I imagine Rahab scurrying around town and casually dropping into each relative's home. In hushed tones, she explains her plan and gives her loved ones specific instructions about what they are and are not to do. She may have disappointed her family with her career choice, but now she's the hero of the hour. They will be safe because of her courage and love when the impending attack becomes a reality. Quiet Rahab, who runs her inn and works in the shadows, is no longer an invisible woman.

....

[80] Joshua 2:15–16.

[81] Joshua 2:17–20.

The escapees proceed as Rahab directs and return to their camp without incident. The report they relay to Joshua, paraphrased, sounds like this: "Woo-hoo, we're good to go! The Lord has given us the entire land, and everyone is terrified because of us!"[82] Their account isn't entirely accurate. Although Rahab, the Beloved Daughter, and her family may feel stressed because of the approaching turmoil, they know they will survive in the end.

In the end—there was a long way to go before that end was in sight. The conquest of Jericho was now underway. Based on the scouts' report, the game was on. The city was locked down, with no one entering or leaving due to the threat from the Israelites. God told Joshua he had given the city, the king, and the "*mighty men of valour*" into their hands,[83] and then he gave Joshua explicit instructions to follow.[84] The description of the army marching around the city and the priests blowing horns is like reading the storyline of an action movie, but God provided the special effects.

And inside that city were Rahab and her family. They were undoubtedly exhausted from the escalating tension, along with everyone else who resided there. The difference for them was that she had tied a scarlet cord in the window, and it was their lifeline—a symbol of Rahab's trust in God.

Let's step into her shoes and envision what's happening from her point of view.

For six days, Rahab hears priests blowing trumpets and the crunch of feet as the Israelite company circles the walls of the city. Very unnerving. And with each pass, the tension among the residents increases. Which day the army will make its move is a mystery to all of them, but Rahab knows the end of the story. She just has no idea how they will get there.

For those six days, Rahab and her family huddle in her home, waiting. The fear is palpable in the room. Some people are sweating, others are jittering, and young children and babies—unable to comprehend the magnitude of the situation—are fussing because of the tension they sense. The bodies are squished together, with each person trying to find a comfortable position in rooms never intended to hold so many. Pungent stress sweat permeates the house. Every muscle in her body is on high alert, ready to jump and guide this group with frayed nerves to safety at a moment's notice.

It was no fairy tale. The situation was dire, but Rahab was a Beloved Daughter awaiting her deliverance. The God who had thrashed cities around her would lead her and her family to safety. She believed that with unwavering certainty.

I get knots in my stomach thinking about the tension and stress that little band experienced, but the faith Rahab evidenced in those circumstances astonishes me.

And then, the seventh day arrives. The Israelite procession begins its circuit at dawn and marches around the city. Inside the house, Rahab sees and hears the army take their lap, and then they do it again and again. She knows something is happening because that's much different from the previous six days. Sensing today may be the day, she gets everyone up, packed, and ready to move.

Joshua has been supervising the march all morning. Then he speaks these words to the Israelites that Rahab knew they would hear: "*And the city and all that is within it shall be devoted to the Lord for destruction* [i.e., be destroyed]. *Only Rahab the prostitute and all who are with her in her house shall live, because she hid the messengers whom we sent.*"[85]

Finally, after the seventh lap, she hears a trumpet blast so loud it feels like her ears will rupture. An enormous shout seems to arise simultaneously from every direction—a noise so thunderous it feels like the earth is moving, and dust fills the air. Pandemonium breaks out everywhere at once. The walls crash, and men climb over the debris and swarm the city.[86] Rahab and her family see and hear it all. The terror, the noise, the shouts, the screams of women and children not knowing where to run, and the coughing and choking as people inhale the dust

....

[85] Joshua 6:17.

[86] Joshua 6:20.

during their flight. Panicked people are everywhere, desperately trying to escape the bedlam and flee the destruction and carnage.

Suddenly, Rahab sees two familiar faces emerge from the chaos. God has pursued her, and Joshua honours the scouts' pact with Rahab and sends those two men to liberate her and her loved ones. There's no question on her part about who they are or why they are there, and they know, without question, whom they seek.[87] Amid the tumult encompassing them, Rahab and her clan are escorted out of the city and ushered to safety outside the Israelite camp.[88]

From her safe vantage point, she stands and watches, mesmerized, as her former home, everything she owned and everyone she knows, perishes in front of her eyes, and the city burns to the ground.[89] As the enormity of it penetrates her consciousness, a sense of deep sadness and grief swirl in the tangle, but relief and joy are also in the mix. God has come through for her.

Rahab and her family escaped annihilation, but that's not the end of the story. She wasn't casually thanked for her service, dismissed, and sent on her way to find a new place to settle and live in peaceful tranquillity, invisible, for the rest of her days. The Israelites gave her a permanent home in their community ever after.[90] A Beloved Daughter.

The first chapter of Matthew in the New Testament details the genealogy of Jesus, and in the line-up, in verse 5, is Rahab. No joking. Rahab, whose name in most places in scripture has the added label "the harlot" or "the prostitute," is one of the ancestors of Jesus. If the burden of your past weighs on you, and you think God can't use you because of something you've done, or someone you were, this is the most encouraging dry reading you may ever do! Rahab wasn't delivered from peril only to fade into obscurity. She became integrated into the Israelite community, and ultimately, she became an ancestor of Jesus. And her accolades don't end there. She's listed in the Hall of Faith in

[87] Joshua 6:22.

[88] Joshua 6:23.

[89] Joshua 6:24.

[90] Joshua 6:25.

Hebrews 11, along with the other heroes of the Bible who exhibited outstanding faith. Let's note that this is not a list of people who simply performed heroic deeds, because the Bible contains many tales of people who accomplished such acts. Only this select few have an eternal place in the Hall of *Faith*.

Hebrews 11:1 gives the biblical definition of faith: "*Now faith is the assurance of things hoped for, the conviction of things not seen*." That means you consider something you believe God will do as a certainty, even if you haven't seen it happen yet. Romans 4:20–21 provides an example of remarkable faith, "*Yet he* [Abraham] *did not waver through unbelief regarding the promise of God, but was strengthened in his faith and gave glory to God, being fully persuaded that God had power to do what he had promised*" (NIV, emphasis added). That's a marked digression from our cultural saying, "Seeing is believing."

God honours faith. Rahab believed God had the power to deliver what his people promised, and God pursued her and honoured her faith by doing just that. She wasn't a worthless puzzle piece to be used and discarded.

Rahab lived the rest of her life as an esteemed member of the Israelite community, no longer invisible. Her label of "Prostitute" was very public, and she couldn't pretend it had never existed. However, although she began as a naughty girl, what she had been in the past no longer mattered. This lady trusted God and accomplished great things for him, regardless of her starting point.

Sometimes the labels that weigh us down are public, as was Rahab's, or self-imposed, or so secret that only we know they're there. Jesus can set you free from the lie that you can never rise above the worst thing you have ever done, and consequently, you must remain invisible and unable to impact your world for him. Rahab didn't happen to catch God on a good day when he was in the mood to help someone. Over and over, the Bible tells us of God's love for us, and it doesn't include the qualifier, "if we …" Yes, he requires things from us as we grow in him, but his love is unconditional. It's that same God who saw and loved this lady from the shadows, and the same God sees and loves you. If you've asked Jesus to forgive you, trust that he has forgiven you. Don't believe the lie that would have you think otherwise. Rahab didn't. Faith and trust were her lifelines, and look what she did for God, despite her background. They are our lifelines too.

This narrative ends with a woman of faith who holds her head high, living a productive life among God's people. And ultimately, she left a remarkable legacy. Invisible? I think not. Beloved Daughter? Most definitely.

5

FROM PERSONAL SUPPORT WIDOW TO BELOVED—RUTH AND NAOMI

Some women have much to endure, and I don't mean spending their vacations camping rather than staying at the Ritz Carlton. In this tale, two ladies had more than their fair share of misery—Ruth and her mother-in-law, Naomi. Losses piled up like cars on an icy highway for Naomi, and although Ruth's losses were fewer, they were significant. When several family members die in a relatively short period, the load of grief is so heavy for the ones left behind that it can be overwhelming. Whether it's one death or several, although others may empathize to a degree, floundering in a world of sadness can leave one feeling alone and invisible. It's not a desirable place to be, but thankfully, God's love can penetrate those places, as these two ladies learned.

This story begins with Naomi's saga, and later Ruth becomes her Personal Support Widow and carries the rest of the narrative. Two invisible women whose lives are intertwined are bound together by love despite their sorrow. They may have begun as invisible, but ultimately, they each take their place as a Beloved Daughter.

Travel with this duo and learn more about a loving God who pursues and reaches out to his Beloved Daughters when life seems to go very wrong.

Naomi, her husband, Elimelech, and their two sons left their hometown of Bethlehem to move to Moab due to famine.[91] Keeping the family from starving superseded living in the same town forever. So not having a bullet train to make the long trip easier, they did what emigrants have done for millennia: packed what they could transport, which didn't likely include her grandmother's china, and started over in a new place. The plan was to *"sojourn"* there,[92] which implies it was a temporary stay, and they would return to their native land in the future, presumably when the fields could again grow food and the supermarket shelves were full.[93]

Tragedy wasn't long in finding Naomi in Moab, because her husband died after they had been there awhile.[94] When a woman walks down the aisle and says, "I do," she believes in the dream of happily ever after. Having it come to an abrupt halt by death through misfortune or illness is rarely something a younger wife sees coming, and Naomi is no exception. Not only was she far from home in a foreign culture, but she was left to care for her two boys alone. Women today are sometimes left in a similar position and struggle to cope with an altered future they neither wanted nor chose. So far from her people, Naomi struggled to work through her grief and fulfill the responsibilities suddenly thrust upon her. Indeed, she was *"a stranger in a strange land"*[95] and must have felt invisible.

[91] Ruth 1:1.

[92] Ruth 1:1.

[93] Block, *Judges, Ruth*, 627.

[94] Ruth 1:3.

[95] Exodus 2:22 (KJV).

There came a season of joy for Naomi when each of her sons married the girl of his dreams, one named Orpah and the other Ruth. The girls weren't Hebrew but natives of her adopted land of Moab. And then tragedy found her again, along with her daughters-in-law. Both sons died.[96] Once more at the graveside there she was, and this time burying her children—an experience no parent would ever wish on anyone. To my mother's heart, it's beyond imagining what it would be like to lose both your husband and your sons and to be the sole survivor of what was once a thriving family. Naomi was older, so there were no more babies destined for her tomorrows even if a new husband came along—unless God decided to perform another Abraham and Sarah wonder, and that was highly unlikely. Sadness shrouded her. Rootless and invisible in a foreign land, she decided it was time to head home, since the fields were again productive.[97] So Naomi began the journey to another new beginning, along with her two daughters-in-law. Let's join her on her way.

As she turns and gazes back at the now familiar landscape, bittersweet memories encompass her on the way out of town. It's Naomi's final farewell to her husband, sons, and dreams for the future, which now lie buried there. She is going home, but it isn't how she anticipated. What emotions are coursing through her mind and soul? Apprehension at what lies ahead, fear, or both mixed with a little joy at returning home? As we previously discussed—in the chapter about the woman who had been hemorrhaging for twelve years—home doesn't remain fixed, so that place of memory doesn't exist in the same way anymore. What awaits them on the other end of the journey?

The trio begins the long trek to Judah. Shortly into their travels, out of consideration, Naomi decides the younger ones should return to their family homes and leave her to continue alone. She doesn't pack them a few falafels and a Twinkie to munch along the way and say, "Nice knowing you." These two companions, who are also grieving the loss of their husbands and happily-ever-afters, have been kind to Naomi.

....

[96] Ruth 1:5.

[97] Ruth 1:6.

Out of love, she blesses them, asks God to return their kindness, and prays they find solace with their families.[98] Releasing them is difficult, particularly since Naomi knows that their company and support would have made her journey more enjoyable. Being women, they have a kiss-and-cry session, but then the pair balk at the plan and decide to stay. Naomi responds by doing what we women often do—that is, try harder if we don't get what we want. This time she objects more forcefully, which leads to another kiss-and-cry—and then Orpah takes her leave.[99]

Ruth does not. Try as she might, Naomi cannot dissuade her daughter-in-law from remaining. Ruth refuses to abandon her dear elder and then utters words that have echoed around the globe at wedding ceremonies, possibly for centuries:

> Do not urge me to leave you or to return from following you. For where you go I will go, and where you lodge I will lodge. Your people shall be my people, and your God my God. Where you die I will die, and there I will be buried …[100]

Ruth speaks these words not to her husband or mother but to her mother-in-law. The depth of love and commitment Ruth extends to Naomi, a woman who has suffered tremendous loss and will soon have to find her place in a world that has changed, was beyond anything even a biological child might demonstrate. And with her declaration, this young woman seals a lifelong pledge to her cherished mother-in-law and places her faith in the one true God. That God has always loved and seen Ruth, and now she has said "yes" to him and become his Beloved Daughter. No longer an invisible woman herself, alone and lost in the maze of her own grief, she belongs to a caring heavenly Father. We will continue with Ruth's part of the story after we explore the rest of Naomi's journey.

....

[98] Ruth 1:8–9.

[99] Ruth 1:9–14.

[100] Ruth 1:16–17.

That same God pursued Naomi and wouldn't let this thoughtful and beloved elder travel home alone, despite her repeated attempts to do so. What thoughts ran through her mind as she tried to process the statement she'd just heard? She too was God's Beloved Daughter, and he provided someone to be her loyal companion who would love her in a way that few people ever experience, apart from the love of a spouse. God saw her, cared about her, and provided for her. She may have continued to feel invisible at times, but he was with her.

Dumbfounded by Ruth's pledge, Naomi wisely keeps silent, and they carry on, eventually arriving at their destination. Bethlehem buzzes with the news that Naomi has returned. There isn't a Welcome Home parade, complete with a marching band in her honour, but something as exciting as Naomi's return to the small community with her daughter-in-law by her side doesn't go unnoticed. People marvel that she has come home. They haven't forgotten her. Naomi doesn't present herself in a movie-character manner—"I'm baaack!"—but the lady whose face bears the story of her tragedies asks those gathered around to call her *Mara*, meaning bitter. It's an appropriate choice of name because it represents the short version of her life.[101] Thankfully, her story doesn't end there. Her loving Father doesn't leave her to wallow in her sorrow with no remedy in sight—he has a plan for both her and Ruth. An adventure is just around the corner that will transform the lives of these two formerly invisible women.

Ruth remains with her mother-in-law day after day as they travel. Having considered her vow before taking it, she does everything within her power to keep it. Thus, she becomes an invaluable companion to the older woman—her Personal Support Widow. The role undoubtedly entails ensuring Naomi doesn't exceed her physical limits, but we know Naomi is a feisty lady.

---

[101] Ruth 1:20–21.

Although Ruth's new position is helpful to her treasured elder, she has left all that is part of her former life—all of her friends, relatives and most possessions—behind. She's heading toward an unknown future, seemingly alone, except for her one companion. But this lady is not invisible; she is a Beloved Daughter of the God she has now chosen to follow, and he will also be with her.

Healing takes place on the long road to Bethlehem. Ruth and Naomi have plenty of time to share memories of their loved ones as they walk each day. Sometimes they laugh, and at other times they cry, as they reminisce about funny and heartwarming stories. Often, words are unnecessary as they lapse into companionable silence. Happy for the company but relaxed enough to retreat into their own thoughts, the long trek deepens their relationship.

Upon arriving in Bethlehem, Ruth assumes the role of breadwinner for them both.[102] Interestingly, she is now an immigrant, something Naomi had experienced a generation earlier when she left her home to start over in a new land. The difference is that Ruth doesn't have children as a tangible reminder of her years with her husband or for companionship in her new life. Feelings of invisibility and loss are probably close to the surface as she works to fit into the new culture. No old friends are waiting to ease her transition, and now she's the "*stranger in a strange land*." But the God who upheld Naomi on her journey, the one Ruth has vowed to follow, is faithful and will help her in this new land too.

It's worth noting that even when a woman becomes a Beloved Daughter and is aware of and fully embraces her identity, those old feelings of invisibility can poke up now and again. While chatting on the phone with a friend I hadn't seen in quite a while, I mentioned this book project. She shared a moving story with me about how God had spoken to her five years earlier and impressed on her that she was a Beloved Daughter. Who knew we had shared a similar experience? Even after that length of time, the telling still brought her to tears, and then she made this poignant comment: "But we forget." Yes, we do, but

---

[102] Ruth 2:2.

thankfully our heavenly Father doesn't, and he embraces us over and over and reassures us of his love.

Ruth doesn't sit around her new home polishing her nails and waiting for someone from the local Holt Renfrew to ring the doorbell and offer her a job. The barley harvest is underway, and she isn't afraid of hard work. Her idea, which Naomi approves, is to gather—or glean—any leftover grain in the fields when the workers have finished harvesting them.[103] Gleaning, with permission, is an acceptable practice for the poor in that culture. It's back-breaking work in the blazing sun, but Ruth is young and willing to suffer any discomfort necessary to care for her mother-in-law and herself. She has a well-established Protestant work ethic, long before there were Protestants.

Ruth "just happens" to find work in a field that belongs to Boaz, who "just happens" to be from her father-in-law, Elimelech's, clan, although that's unknown to her at the time.[104] Don't you love divine appointments that at first glance appear to be coincidences? Boaz arrives at the field, greets his workers, and then asks the foreman who the lovely young lady is toiling behind the reapers.[105] No matter how she currently perceives herself, that lovely young lady is not invisible.

Once he knows Ruth's family ties and receives the report from the field manager that she's a diligent worker, Boaz invites her to glean in his fields and asks her not to work elsewhere.[106] From the outset, he assumes the role of her protector and instructs her to stay close to the women working in the fields. They will provide companionship and group protection, something a newcomer to that line of work may not have considered. Additionally, Boaz reads the riot act to the young men to leave Ruth alone, implying their intentions toward her may have been less than honourable. Then he welcomes her with grace and generosity and offers her access to the workers' drinking water, which is an enormous kindness because it means she won't have to haul a heavy

....

[103] Ruth 2:2.

[104] Ruth 2:3.

[105] Ruth 2:5.

[106] Ruth 2:8.

jug from home each morning. The bonus for Ruth is that he instructs those same young men to draw the water for her.[107] For someone who knows no one in the community, Boaz's help is invaluable, especially since it's only her first day of work. Many key details "just happen" to fall into place for her, and we can see the hand of God working in the background, supporting his Beloved Daughter.

Incredulous at Boaz's offer, Ruth throws herself on the dusty ground, humbly bows before him, and asks what she has done to deserve such kindness, especially since she's a foreigner. His answer is noteworthy: her reputation has preceded her.[108] The Bethlehem Communication System is functioning splendidly. The story of Ruth's love for Naomi and leaving her extended family to care for her mother-in-law has made the circuit in record time. She doesn't boast about her decision on Facebook—her love speaks volumes all by itself, and God honours her faithfulness.

Boaz blesses Ruth and invites her to eat with his reapers at break time, a veritable feast compared with what she has stashed in her pack. Afterwards, he implements a strategy to help her glean in a way that will be less physically demanding but still keep her dignity intact by allowing her to contribute some effort to the task.[109]

At daybreak, Ruth is an independent figure in the field, but by the end of the day, this new immigrant is a member of a ladies' club, The Women of the Sheaves. She even has a benefactor who keeps the boys in line. It's been the first day of a new job worth celebrating. Just as God saw Hagar, God sees Ruth and has prepared a place for her. All she has to do is trust him.

Delighted that she's had a productive shift and that her day turned out so well, Ruth speeds home that evening with light steps. Then, with an even lighter heart, she presents Naomi with the day's gleanings. Along with the grain is a treat nestled in her bag for her elder—the extra food from her gourmet lunch the newly employed worker had tucked

....

[107] Ruth 2:9.

[108] Ruth 2:10–11.

[109] Ruth 2:12, 14–16.

away.[110] Thoughtfulness is part of Ruth's makeup. Even in reduced circumstances, she delights in extending hospitality to bless her mother-in-law. As they amiably chat about the day, Naomi expresses gratitude for the man who allowed Ruth to work in his fields.

Bitterness and resentment could have enveloped both women; however, they chose thankfulness instead. Hard times are anything but fun, but soft hearts are fertile ground for God to cultivate. With the seeds of gratitude and appreciation, these Beloved Daughters allowed God to produce prize-worthy botanical gardens from their lives.

It gets even better. Ruth's jaw drops when Naomi reveals Boaz's full identity to her. That nice man isn't just a kind stranger but a close relative from her husband's line and a *redeemer*.[111] That's amazing! What's a redeemer?

A long treatise on the role of a redeemer, sometimes called a kinsman-redeemer, isn't necessary, but a short explanation will help us understand why it was significant. Edward Woods states in *Deuteronomy: An Introduction and Commentary*:

> The main idea behind the practice [of kinsman-redeemership] is that, if a man died without a male heir, it was the duty of his brother to marry his widow and produce a son, who would then inherit the deceased brother's name and property. The practice ensured that property would remain *within the family*, and that the dead brother's *name* would be carried forward for posterity.[112]

The IVP Bible Background Commentary: Old Testament defines the brother as the nearest male kin.[113] The law in Deuteronomy also provided

---

[110] Ruth 2:18.

[111] Ruth 2:20.

[112] Woods, *Deuteronomy: An Introduction and Commentary*, 257.

[113] Matthews et al., *The IVP Bible Background Commentary: Old Testament*, electronic ed., Dt 25:5–10.

the right of refusal to that relative if he were unwilling or unable to fulfill his duty.[114]

How did this practice relate to Ruth? Elimelech didn't have an heir, which is why the two ladies found themselves in this challenging situation. Naomi was too old to have more babies, so Ruth was the designated survivor to rescue the family by marrying again and producing a son.[115] Hence, Boaz, being a redeemer and a really nice man was a win-win for the ladies. (He certainly didn't complain about it, judging by his apparent interest in Ruth.)

Until the end of the harvest, Ruth slogs away gleaning with the ladies' club, and her darkened skin bears testimony to the hours she spends in the beating sun.[116] Naomi has been pondering their next steps, and when there's no more work in the fields, she informs Ruth it's time to take action and secure her future well-being.[117] Ruth's response may have been "Yesss!" or "Uh oh," but she allows the older woman to advise her either way.

Having been raised in the Hebrew culture, Naomi is aware of the practices associated with the redemption process. But in addition to having that knowledge, she's a wise lady. She could play the victim and demand the appointed relative step up and accept his legal responsibility; however, she chooses a more prudent approach. Humility.[118]

After listening to her elder's proposition, Ruth voices her acceptance. She doesn't merely comply and leave the door open for recriminations later should things not work out.[119] As instructed, she cleans herself up, adds a little splash of Chanel No. 5, puts on her best outfit, and heads to the threshing floor, where her potential husband is working.

Older women who understand the ways of men know a thing or two about timing. Naomi realizes that the time Boaz will most likely be receptive to the overture Ruth is primed to make will be after din-

....

[114] Deuteronomy 25:5–10.

[115] Ruth 4:5.

[116] Ruth 2:23.

[117] Ruth 3:1–4.

[118] Guzik, "Ruth 3—Ruth Makes an Appeal," *Enduring Word Bible Commentary,* A.2.b(ii0).

[119] Ruth 3:5.

ner. Tired, hungry, and possibly grumpy does not set the scene for an intimate chat. So Ruth keeps out of Boaz's sight and doesn't approach him until he hunkers down for the night after dinner, and "*his heart* [is] *merry.*"[120] The older lady did know a thing or two.

In substance, Ruth's next actions propose marriage to Boaz. Cautiously, she lifts the blanket off his feet and, trying not to disturb him, quietly slips under it and covers herself.[121] No doubt, sleep evades her because her thoughts are racing. Her anxiety level is clocking in at an eleven on a scale of one to ten. *How will he react? Is she about to suffer humiliation in addition to all she has already endured?* Every time he moves in his sleep, her heart probably skips a beat. *Has the moment arrived?*

Something startles him at midnight (his snoring?), and judging by his response, finding a woman at his feet isn't an everyday occurrence. Saying that is an understatement doesn't come close to describing the situation. She can't miss his amazement when he discovers her and asks who she is.[122] No street lights penetrate the darkness, and presumably he has a few cobwebs to clear from his sleepy brain to make sense of the situation. Ruth quickly identifies herself and then reveals her motivation.[123] *Will he accept his role as her redeemer?* He is alert immediately, and his kind eyes and soft words convey his delight that she has chosen him, an older man, not a rich or poor handsome young lad.[124] That declaration does wonders to reduce some of her apprehension and allows hope to begin to seep into her soul. She is not invisible. God has a relief plan for her and her dear mother-in-law.

But there's a snag. Right. Doesn't it seem as if there's usually a snag when the desired result is within reach? Unfortunately, not much in life runs smoothly, and here's another instance in which she must trust God through the bumps. Having been on tenterhooks that Boaz will accept

[120] Ruth 3:7.
[121] Ruth 3:7.
[122] Ruth 3:9.
[123] Ruth 3:9.
[124] Ruth 3:10.

her, she barely has a chance to exhale when another issue surfaces. Life sometimes feels like a roller coaster, and she experiences that feeling first-hand; however, trust develops on the wild ride. God has brought her this far, and although she can't overcome all the obstacles herself, he can.

The unfortunate bump in the road is that as much as Boaz wants to redeem her, he's second in line—another relative has the right of first refusal.[125] Suddenly, Ruth's future, which seemed to be heading in the right direction only a heartbeat before, is again in question. The goal of having a redeemer make everything right with the world appears to be a moving target at that moment, and reaching it is outside her control. She lets out her breath to calm her racing nerves and pays full attention to his explanation. If the other person (let's call him Mystery Man #1, or MM #1 for short) is willing to assume his responsibility as the redeemer, Boaz must say goodbye to what looks like a delightful future. But if not, then he will be thrilled to accept Ruth's proposal. Boaz promises to resolve the problem in the morning, so he tells her to sleep for the rest of the night because they can't do anything about it now.[126]

How does that work for you? Your future is hanging in the balance, but relax, take a nap, and tomorrow you'll know whether the landowner or the mystery man behind door #1 will be your husband. I don't think counting all the sheep in the universe would knock me out after that discussion.

Ruth doesn't run away screaming or burst into tears but leaves the problem with Boaz, prudently aware of what is within her control and what is not. Then she lets God do the rest. This Beloved Daughter is a wise lady too.

Time for a disclaimer: kids, don't try this at home, or anywhere else for that matter! Bizarre as the redeemer custom seems to twenty-first-century readers, it was perfectly acceptable at the time. It's not applicable in today's culture, so don't even think about making a case for it being a biblical precedent to follow.

....

[125] Ruth 3:12.

[126] Ruth 3:13.

The next day before it's light, Boaz scuttles Ruth off so she won't become the talk of the town, sending her home with a gift of barley for Naomi.[127] What a thoughtful man! The older woman is waiting in suspense, and when Ruth arrives, she can see the anxiety etched on her face. What happened? After Ruth relays the details, Naomi responds with the voice of reason: "He isn't going to rest until it's sorted out today, so settle down."[128] Older women in the Bible sound just like mothers do today.

Boaz wastes no time and hurries to the city gates, where the men conduct business. He waits until he spots Mystery Man #1. Along with a group of city elders, he invites him to join an official chat. Boaz then lays out the necessity for a redeemer for Elimelech's family. He explains that MM #1 is the family's closest relative, so he's first in line for the redeemer job. Happy to oblige, MM #1 is willing to accept his responsibility and redeem the land until Boaz throws in the minor detail that Ruth comes along with the deal.[129] Sly fox that he is, he holds that tidbit back to slip in at the end for a satisfying "Gotcha!" Undoubtedly, Boaz enjoys watching the man squirm and backpedal as fast as he can. MM #1 knows that if he were to marry Ruth and father an heir for Elimelech, he would alter the inheritance structure for his own children. So in an instant, he passes the responsibility to Redeemer #2, Boaz, whose eyes sparkle.[130] Everything is done according to the Robert's Rules of Order of the day, and the shoe ceremony seals the contract in front of ten city elders. Everyone in the group, including the elders, gives the final "aye."[131] That isn't quite the end of the meeting, though. All the people who pass the vote charge Boaz to live honourably and confer a blessing on him and Ruth, their home and offspring.[132] What an excellent foundation on which to build a godly home.

....

[127] Ruth 3:14–15, 17.

[128] Ruth 3:18 (paraphrased).

[129] Ruth 4:1–5.

[130] Ruth 4:6.

[131] Ruth 4:7–11.

[132] Ruth 4:11–12.

A splashy wedding, complete with the bride wearing a fluffy confection, isn't what they choose. They marry quickly and quietly,[133] and Naomi sports the most enormous smile her face has worn in years.

Subsequently, to the delight of the new family unit, Ruth conceives a child and, in time, bears a son.

Looking back over her life, it's unlikely Ruth would have willingly chosen the trajectory her life took, but God saw, pursued, and blessed her beyond her wildest imaginings. She was not invisible to him but a Beloved Daughter he entrusted with a hard journey. Growth happens in places we don't like—the difficult places. Yet despite her grief and uncertainty concerning the future, Ruth left behind all that was familiar, accepted responsibility for her mother-in-law, and loved and cared for her in an exceptional way. God blessed her commitment and forever elevated her to a place of honour.

Ruth began as an invisible woman, but she doesn't remain that way—God saw and pursued her. And the ending of her story is worth celebrating. The short version of her life is that she was a daughter-in-law, became a widow, accepted the role of Personal Support Widow for the elder she cherished, and chose to become a Beloved Daughter of God. Eventually, she married Boaz and bore a son, Obed, who became the father of Jesse, King David's father. So that made her the great-grandmother of King David, from whose line Jesus was born, and Jesus came to redeem the world. Breathtaking, isn't it?

Naomi's story ended well too, even though she began as an invisible woman, pitched into a world of personal tragedy. After great hardship in her life, the ladies in her community were ecstatic when she became a grandmother. God's goodness was writ large in her life, and they knew he was with her:

---

[133] Ruth 4:13.

Blessed be the Lord, who has not left you this day without a redeemer, and may his name be renowned in Israel. He shall be to you a restorer of life and a nourisher of your old age, for your daughter-in-law who loves you, who is more to you than seven sons, has given birth to him.[134]

God had seen Naomi's pain and suffering and pursued her, providing a beloved daughter-in-law for her difficult journey despite this dear woman's attempts to thwart his plan. In sending a redeemer to these ladies' rescue, he secured their financial future. In addition to living to see her grandson born, Naomi became his nurse[135] and spent time every day enjoying the miracle God had given her.

The God who had his hand upon her through the tough years, the years when she felt invisible, brought everything together in the end and tied it up with a big bow for this Beloved Daughter.

The Psalms were written much later, but this passage seems appropriate to their journey: "*Your* (God's) *path led through the sea, your way through the mighty waters, though your footprints were not seen.*"[136] God's footprints didn't always show on the path these women travelled, but he did lead them to Boaz, a redeemed future, and into life as Beloved Daughters.

God is in control even if your journey has taken a course that wouldn't be your first choice, like Naomi and Ruth's. You might feel unseen and not recognize his footprints, but he is pursuing you, and he sees and loves you and will lead you through the sea, Beloved Daughter. And you may have water wings to share with others when you reach the shore.

....

[134] Ruth 4:14–15.

[135] Ruth 4:16.

[136] Psalm 77:19 (NIV).

6

FROM CINDERELLA TO BELOVED —HANNAH

Have you ever encountered someone who seemed to live a true-life Cinderella story? Or maybe you've felt like you were the Cinderella, invisible to the world, with an evil stepmother or equivalent who enjoyed making your life miserable? Meet Hannah. She seemed to have the starring role in a fairy tale, but it wasn't a part anyone would relish. Her reality wasn't pleasant, which is an understatement, but God intervened and transformed her life. He saw an invisible, heart-broken lady in gruelling circumstances and walked with this Beloved Daughter on her life journey. Let's examine Hannah's experience and see what she learned about travelling a challenging path, not alone, but with an extraordinary God. That same God's eyes and heart are set on you too.

Elkanah is a gentleman we meet at the beginning of 1 Samuel, and it doesn't take a gifted intellect to figure out that he had a problem. Check it out: "*He had two wives. The name of the one was Hannah, and the name of the other, Peninnah. And Peninnah had children, but Hannah had no children.*"[137]

There we have it—he was the lucky husband of not one but two wives; one had kids, and the other did not. It sounds like the framework for anything but family peace and harmony. Unfortunately for Hannah, she was the "did not" wife.

Life wasn't easy or happy for Hannah, although neither is a given in this world. Each morning, her struggles greeted her as she began her day. The culture she lived in prized childbearing and considered it a woman's primary role. Hence, no offspring, no status—the perfect set-up for feelings of invisibility to germinate.

Every time she ventured out into public to shop or worship, she endured sidelong glances from other women in her wake as she passed. Some had sympathy on their faces, but an attitude of superiority or even judgment seemed to exude from others. Being unable to live up to social expectations and, consequently, being an object of pity or disdain is no one's idea of a good time. The label attached to Hannah's name wasn't likely a positive attribute such as charming or kind, but barren. And for Hannah, it wasn't a party. The meaning of "*the Lord had closed her womb*"[138] is uncertain, so cause aside, the reality was that she couldn't have babies.

Women have wrestled with infertility in every generation for millennia, and the feelings involved remain relatively unchanged. A young woman told me the story of her difficulty conceiving and the multiple miscarriages she's experienced. Her pain is deep, but she has permitted me to share some of those feelings of grief and despair that enveloped her. Her experience brings Hannah's struggle to life and gives us a glimpse into the pain women in similar straits endure.

This young lady told me that hope turned into disappointment month after month until, at last, she knew the thrill of conceiving. However,

[137] 1 Samuel 1:2.

[138] 1 Samuel 1:5.

her joy was short-lived and followed by the devastation of first learning the baby she carried wouldn't survive and then grief when it ultimately did not. And then the cycle of monthly disappointment as she tried to conceive, eventually becoming pregnant and losing the baby, happened again. And again. Grief upon grief was carried quietly between husband and wife because it was too personal, too intimate, to share. All the while, she had to cope with questions like, "When are you going to start a family?" Finally she carried a baby to term and delivered a healthy boy, but the cycle began again when they tried for a second child.

That was one part of her experience. The other was when her friends conceived children. Of course, she wanted to be happy for them, but her broken heart cried, "*What about me?*"

Unless we've experienced something similar, I don't think we can comprehend the soul-crushing process of trying and failing to conceive or carry a baby to term, which can continue for years for some couples. Because it's such a private journey, hidden from even family and close friends, the women caught in it can feel alone and invisible.

Hannah would have experienced those same feelings as she watched her husband's other wife bear child after child, and each one reinforced the message that she wasn't enough. She was defective, the wife who couldn't and didn't measure up to expectations of her, invisible. Unfortunately, it was impossible to fix the ailment herself. Like the hemorrhaging woman, Hannah had a problem not of her own making but ultimately bore the consequences of it.

The biblical account of Hannah's saga begins as she accompanies her husband and the rest of the clan on his annual trip to Shiloh to sacrifice to the Lord.[139] It's no vacation at Disney World for her, though. A good time is not had by all. After he offers his sacrifice, Elkanah returns with some meat for the family and does what any wise dad might do. He feeds Peninnah and the kids first because hungry kids can be cranky kids, and nobody enjoys being around cranky kids.

That sounds like a perfectly reasonable arrangement, but there's more to the story. First Samuel 1:5 says, "*But to Hannah, he gave a double*

---

[139] 1 Samuel 1:3.

portion because he loved her ..." Although the interpretation of the portion size varies from version to version of the Bible, the motivation behind his choice is the critical point. Elkanah loved Hannah. The scripture doesn't note that he also loved Peninnah. That distinction implies his feelings for his second wife were not as strong, creating the perfect set-up for friction. Two women each desired the affection of the same man, and one had the family he wanted, while the other held his heart.

Although they don't scratch out each other's eyes, and Peninnah doesn't try to slip poison into Hannah's coffee in the morning, she doesn't play nicely with Hannah. First Samuel 1:6 says, "*And her rival used to provoke her grievously to irritate her because the Lord had closed her womb.*" Hannah has to deal with the sorrow and despair resulting from her infertility, plus the additional anguish when another woman uses her situation as a weapon to torment her emotionally. Peninnah doesn't just have a superior attitude toward Hannah as she gloats about her own good fortune. This unkind co-wife "*provoke[s] her grievously,*" which means the woman is downright nasty. It isn't a temporary situation or an isolated incident; she torments her *every single year.*[140] Theirs is not a happy home. The extent of the nastiness inflicted by Peninnah screams jealousy and an awareness of her inferior position to the wife cherished in her husband's affections.

There is Hannah, in a contentious relationship, enduring the most horrible church camp experience every year. What recourse does she have? Does she feel like Cinderella with a cruel stepmother taunting and driving her? Does she want to hide in a corner by the fireplace and sing Disney songs to escape her misery? Rather than sinking into a pit of anger and bitterness, she lives with a broken heart, an ongoing open wound. Although Hannah's husband loves her, life is thorny, and she is hidden in the background and must feel invisible in a world that revolves around family. First Samuel 1:7 says she "*wept and would not eat.*" Some women in emotional distress eat to relieve the pain, and some lose their appetite and struggle to eat anything. Even chocolate. Hard to imagine, but true. Hannah falls into the "don't even make me think about food

---

[140] 1 Samuel 1:7.

when I am this unhappy" category. Her husband tries to console her, but even that's not enough to soothe the heartbreak that consumes her.

Have you ever felt like Hannah, as though a brick wall is in front of you and there's no one to help? Hidden away and alone in your distress? Wisely, Hannah doesn't unload her misery to Facebook or fight Peninnah in a knock-down-drag-out battle to the death. Instead, she heads to the temple and weeps bitter tears before the Lord.[141] God is the only one who can help her, so quietly, this desperate soul pours her heart out to him in that place of worship. Her body is still, with only her lips moving as she delivers her petition.

Eli, the priest, watches closely. When Hannah glances upward, she sees an expression of disgust on his face, and he accuses her of being drunk.[142] Talk about adding insult to injury! On her family "vacation" with the evil co-wife who makes life pure misery year after year, when she has one opportunity to escape the fray and bare her soul to the Lord, the spiritual leader accuses her of being intoxicated. Compassion and understanding would have gone a long way in helping her, but instead, he misinterprets her actions. The priest judges her for something she didn't do, and, in addition, he treats her with contempt.

Hannah is utterly invisible. Her character, needs, desires, and wounds are far from the priest's awareness. In a similar situation, I may have had to bite back a retort like, "I'm *praying*!" But to her credit, she gives a soft answer and says, "*Do not regard your servant as a worthless woman,*" after explaining she is not drunk but is praying because of her deep emotional distress.[143] A "worthless woman," indeed.

Being misunderstood and judged by someone who should support you is upsetting. And the entire direction of Hannah's life might have changed from that moment on had she allowed bitterness to grow in her heart toward Peninnah and spill out onto the insensitive Eli. But she is resilient and chooses to use her voice rather than slink into silent despair or nurse another wound. She stands up to him and clarifies what she's

---

[141] 1 Samuel 1:10.

[142] 1 Samuel 1:12–14.

[143] 1 Samuel 1:15–16.

doing. He accepts her explanation, asks God to grant her request, and then sends her on her way with a blessing.[144] But had Hannah left angry because someone heaped another injustice upon her, she might have forfeited that blessing, and Eli may never have uttered his prayer.

After that experience, something happens to Hannah; the weight she has shouldered for so long lifts, and she is starving. The deep etching of sadness on her face also disappears.[145] She has connected with God. At this point, her circumstances haven't changed in any way. Everything in her life seems to be the same as before her God moment. So what's different? Her focus has changed. When God touches her wounded soul, joy returns and shines on her face and through her eyes; she is ready for a Big Mac and to resume her roles and responsibilities. An encounter with God can do that, and Hannah has just entered the realm of a Beloved Daughter, a secure place. Her security isn't dependent on results but on a relationship, and she walks away with a new awareness of who her God is.

What was the prayer she offered when she entered God's presence? It wasn't a selfish, "Please God, let me have a baby so I can be happy and not scorned or judged anymore" kind of prayer. It was a thoughtful petition and offered at an immense personal cost:

> And she made a vow, saying, "Lord Almighty, if you will only look on your servant's misery and remember me, and not forget your servant but give her a son, then I will give him to the Lord for all the days of his life, and no razor will ever be used on his head."[146]

The scripture says Hannah "*vowed*," which is a binding promise, not a passing whim quickly forgotten. Vows are serious in the Bible, so she didn't take it lightly, and she was aware of the price she would pay when God answered. This lady was committed to upholding her pledge from

---

[144] 1 Samuel 1:17.

[145] 1 Samuel 1:18.

[146] 1 Samuel 1:11 (NIV).

the beginning because there wasn't room for, "Oh, sorry, I changed my mind. I want to keep my son. Thanks anyway." The petition was for God to grant her a son; if he did, she would return the child to God for lifelong service in the temple. She also vowed he would be a Nazirite, which her promise "*no razor will ever be used on his head*" means. The Nazirite vow involved the three elements outlined in Numbers 6.[147] The arrangement she offered God wasn't for shared custody—this determined woman was willing to surrender her son completely so that God might fulfill his purposes in the child's life.

What a promise. Many of us dearly want children, and when they come into our family, we hold them tightly and enjoy the completeness they bring to our lives. Can you imagine going into that mother-child relationship, one you had dreamed about for years, aware you had limited time to enjoy your child before releasing him to the care of others? And you came up with the idea of handing him over to the Lord forever yourself!

When the birds start greeting the world the morning after her prayer in the temple, Hannah and her husband worship together, pack their gear, load their vehicle, and head home. Back home on the range, they have a delightful time together, and something amazing happens. Well, something other than just a delightful time. First Samuel 1:19b says, "… *and the Lord remembered her*." That statement is breathtaking. God remembers the brokenhearted woman who has suffered much and been invisible for so many years. *He remembers* his Beloved Daughter.

And then she conceives a son. Imagine the excitement Hannah experiences when she realizes her years of monthly disappointment are finally over and she will become a mother! Once she knows it's a certainty, she probably traipses up and down the streets sporting maternity clothes, possibly sooner than necessary, collecting all the baby equipment

[147] "The Hebrew term for 'Nazirite' comes from the Hebrew word meaning "to separate." Numbers 6 presents the distinguishing features of the vow as:
- abstaining from anything related to grapes and/or alcohol
- refraining from cutting one's hair
- avoiding dead people (even family members.)" (Franklin, "Nazarite," *The Lexham Bible Dictionary*, electronic ed.).

she can locate. Then she settles into nesting mode, sews and knits the clothing she has fantasized about for years, and creates the most elaborate layette ever seen on earth. At least, that's how I picture it. Finally she will have a baby, and while he is hers to nurture, she will savour the process. Every scent (some definitely sweeter than others), sound (some more agreeable than others), and experience (some more pleasant than others) will be precious, even if she doesn't sleep much for a few short years. She will store those images in the treasure chest of her memory because it's the stuff of her dreams.

God remembered this lady who began as a tormented co-wife. He saw and acted on her behalf. She was not invisible.

As a woman of honour, Hannah keeps her vow. After her son, whom she names Samuel, arrives, she foregoes the family's annual trek to sacrifice to the Lord but understands the deferral is for a limited time. From the beginning of her son's life, she accepts the boundaries she has created for her role and tells her husband, *"As soon as the child is weaned, I will bring him, so that he may appear in the presence of the Lord and dwell there forever."*[148] There is no definitive information in scripture about Samuel's age when his life at the temple begins other than this statement in 1 Samuel 1:24b: *"And the child was young."* In *1 and 2 Samuel: An Introduction and Commentary*, Long says, "In the Ancient Near East, children were typically weaned at about three years of age."[149] Samuel left home at a remarkably tender age if Hannah followed this practice.

Hannah and Elkanah eventually take Samuel to the temple and present him to Eli, reminding the old priest about who she is and the promise she once made. Then in a supreme act of self-sacrifice, with great anguish, she surrenders the boy to Eli's care. But deep in her being is a ripple of joy because she has a son she can give to God. Forever. She clearly states that because the Lord granted her petition, she is now lending Samuel to the Lord for as long as he lives.[150] That was her promise, and she is honouring it. Yet although Hannah has always

---

[148] 1 Samuel 1:22.

[149] Long, *1 and 2 Samuel: An Introduction and Commentary*, 44.

[150] 1 Samuel 1:25–28.

known this day would come, I suspect that because she's also human and a mother, it's still excruciating to wave goodbye to her son and walk away to return to a quieter house with a big hole in her heart.

Feeling like she has left part of her soul behind, Hannah doesn't walk away with her head down and feet dragging, thinking about her misery. Instead, she prays because she knows a secret in the spiritual realm about dealing with stress and emotional upset. Hers isn't a "Woe is me. I've just relinquished my cherished son, and I don't know how I will ever cope" kind of prayer. No, this resilient woman lifts her voice in praise and exaltation to the God she loves and declares, *"My heart exults in the Lord …"*[151] And then she joyfully proclaims the awesome things God does. She praises him with her whole being, *"There is none holy like the Lord: for there is none besides you; there is no rock like our God."*[152] Hannah's lifeline is focusing on God and not on her issues, and she knows the value of praise in maintaining that focus.

We sing those words in worship today, words Hannah composed more than two thousand years ago. That's quite the reach for someone who began as Cinderella. The time of closeness between mother and child was over, but her relationship with God was anything but. This lady's strength came from the Lord because she knew that the God who granted her prayer would continue caring for her. This Beloved Daughter's security was in him.

Each year afterwards, when these parents visit their boy during their excursion to offer sacrifices, Hannah delivers a little robe she has made for Samuel and his work in the temple. See, she was a seamstress and probably did make a layette for Baby Samuel! In preparing to sew his annual gift, every fabric store in town is probably on her list to visit, each bolt of cloth caressed until she finds the one perfect for his tender skin. Then as Hannah works, I see her pouring her heart into every stitch and not being satisfied until each one is perfect. Since she only visits her son once a year, she wants to be sure the one item she creates for him won't be one he examines repeatedly and thinks, *You missed a stitch here, Mom.*

....

[151] 1 Samuel 2:1a.

[152] 1 Samuel 2:2.

This mother does her best for her treasured son, and as she works, she prays that God will bless and use him in his ministry in the temple.

Can you imagine Samuel's excitement as he anticipates his parents' arrival? Surely he misses them as much as they miss him, and he also knows that his mother will bring a new creation for him to wear each year. I don't think his attitude is, "Oh dear, I have to wear something Mom made me. Again." He probably longs for the visit with his parents during their lengthy absences and looks forward to the ritual with great delight. Each work of art his mother brings is a tangible expression of her love for him, one that will remain long after she departs.

As part of their annual tradition, Eli, the priest, blesses Elkanah and Hannah and says, *"May the Lord give you children by this woman for the petition she asked of the Lord."*[153] Eli knows he benefits from Hannah's promise by having Samuel working at the temple. In turn, he asks God to give the couple more little ones. God pursues Hannah, answers that prayer, and exuberantly blesses her and her husband by giving them more bundles of joy. Interestingly, when Hannah made her vow to God, she didn't know that he would give her more children. She asked for a son and was prepared to return him to the Lord with no conditions attached.

Three more sons and two daughters are how God blesses them, which means changing scores of diapers over the years, but also a household filled with joy. The formerly invisible Hannah goes from being infertile to becoming a mother of six children. It all starts with a prayer of faith and the integrity to keep her oath. God honours that faith and trustworthiness by giving her six times what she requests. Occasionally, I fear that what God is asking is too costly, and I struggle to obey. But Hannah's story reveals the greatness of a God who gives far more than he asks.

Releasing Samuel for his work in the temple is not likely a one-and-done situation for Hannah. Yes, she knows the power of praise and that she is a Beloved Daughter, but when this mother has a few minutes to sit by the fire and sew, I think her heart and mind wander to Samuel again

....

[153] 1 Samuel 2:20a.

and again. When the longing surfaces, chances are she has to surrender him to the Lord again, and I'm sure praise is the balm for her soul each time. Eventually it probably becomes easier, but I suspect it's a process, not a single occurrence.

That's life. There aren't many situations where everything gets neatly resolved all at once, at least not for me. Sometimes I need to recommit something I've already entrusted to the Lord, which can be difficult, even though it isn't the first time I've walked that path.

This tale began with Hannah as a Cinderella figure, consistently and deliberately being provoked by her husband's other wife about her inability to have children, even though she was the cherished wife. Consequently, she felt invisible, leaving her with a choice to make. This tormented woman could have withdrawn and wallowed in the injustice of her situation. But instead, she chose to take her place as a Beloved Daughter by trusting God with her life. In taking the second option, Hannah left her world of invisibility and dared to place her future in his hands. It wasn't easy, but it was worth it, and everything changed when God entered the picture.

If Hannah intimidates you because it seems that she lived on a much higher plane than you do, and that even in stressful situations she made all the right choices, let's look at her narrative from a different perspective. Her story isn't a highlights reel, as you might see on social media, with all the hard parts omitted, but it's condensed into two chapters, so along with what is said, much is left unsaid. No doubt she didn't always respond to her tormentor with the milk of human kindness. Real women are not paragons of virtue every minute of every day, and Hannah was a real woman. The Bible didn't record her story to set a standard impossible for us to attain. Instead, it's a testament to her faith and God's love. We can learn from the secrets Hannah discovered—like the power of praise and drawing strength from God as we grow in our faith.

Although Hannah received the answer to her prayer that she requested, and the young lady I mentioned earlier ultimately did have a second child, that isn't always how it turns out. Hannah's story isn't a formula for curing infertility. When she left the temple with a joyful heart, knowing she had connected with God, she couldn't foresee how her tale would end. But she knew she was the Beloved Daughter of the one who held that ending in his hands.

I have no idea why God answers the prayer for children for some women, and for others, what seems like Plan B becomes their permanent detour. And I'm not about to present trite platitudes to you Beloved Daughters who live with that pain. However, whether it's infertility or another seemingly insurmountable obstacle in your path, I can point you to the same one who loved and cared for Hannah, because he cares for you.[154]

One friend of mine and her husband were unable to have children, and she's had to deal with the why for many years. The loss she feels is ongoing because, in her words, "it really never goes away." There's a beautiful "but" to her story, however. Through her and her husband's careers, God has opened remarkable avenues for them to be in relationships with other people's children, and their influence will be felt for generations. She admits, "It wasn't our Plan A, but we don't feel like it's a Plan B either. It's simply God's plan for our lives. It's not even the career that brings me joy—it's that [it] places me in the lives of so many young adults that I would never have had access to without [it]."

She doesn't discount the reality of the hole in their lives that has remained with being childless. "It's definitely not our preferred side of the coin. [However], it's very important to realize that even when our prayers remain unanswered, it doesn't mean God loves us any less. It just means that we don't know the full story he's writing with our lives—and we may not know until eternity. It doesn't make him any less faithful—and it doesn't make us any less loved—it just makes us people who are *bought with a price*"[155] and, therefore, not their own."[156] That statement

---

[154] 1 Peter 5:7.

[155] 1 Corinthians 6:20.

[156] I Corinthians 6:19.

is powerful from someone who has chosen to walk in faith and trust, even though she lives daily with a sizeable unknown. Isaiah 55:8–9 puts it into perspective: *"For my thoughts are not your thoughts, neither are your ways my ways, declares the Lord. For as the heavens are higher than the earth, so are my ways higher than your ways and my thoughts than your thoughts."*

If we keep our focus locked on what we want, and the outcome isn't what we planned, we can live in disappointment and miss the opportunities God has for us. But trust leads to freedom—freedom to live with unanswered questions and not be immobilized by them. There may be an exciting new beginning just around the corner, but we won't find it if we refuse to forge ahead.

We are not Beloved Daughters because our lives turn out the way we plan. We are Beloved Daughters because God loves us so much that he sent his son to die for us, regardless of our circumstances. When we believe in him, he walks with us every step of the way. We are not invisible or forgotten; we are Beloved Daughters of the Most High God, and come what may, we can face it because he is there. Zechariah 10:11–12 says, *" 'They will pass through the sea of trouble; the surging sea will be subdued … I will strengthen them in the Lord and in his name they will live securely,' declares the Lord"* (NIV). He is the God who can move you and me from invisible to beloved, and we can live securely in that new identity. His strength is enough to lead us through whatever seas we encounter.

7

FROM TRICKED AND TRADED TO BELOVED—LEAH AND RACHEL

Remaining single may be disappointing, and you might feel overlooked if your heart is set on finding the love of your life and riding off into the sunset together. What we rarely consider in our dreams is how complicated love and life can become after the sunset. If ever there was a tangled love story, Jacob, Rachel, and Leah's tale is the one. It wasn't just a case of man met woman, decided to marry woman, and did. It was a disaster because it turned into a love triangle, which was not of their own doing.

There were two invisible women in this narrative. Their Dear Old Dad tricked their husband into marrying the wrong sister by trading the desired one, Rachel, for the less desirable one, Leah, on the wedding night. Shortly after that, the groom also married the sought-after sister, resulting in one husband and two wives—a complicated situation. Leah wasn't physically dazzling and became the unloved, invisible wife. The gorgeous and treasured wife, Rachel, felt invisible because she couldn't bear children. Their lives were inextricably linked, but we'll focus most of our discussion on Leah. However, God was in control, and he saw and loved both of these Beloved Daughters in their distress. Delve into their tale to build your faith and trust in the same caring God who sees our hardships and reaches out to us in love too.

The household buzzed and rumours flew. Jacob had arrived from somewhere far away and was staying with his uncle, Laban. The word was that Jacob's arrival had something to do with stealing his brother's blessing and needing a quick getaway to escape his wrath. The grapevine also reported that Jacob planned to find a wife while he was there.[157]

After a month, Jacob had settled in and was well-established in the household.[158] Behind closed doors, Laban negotiated a financial agreement with his nephew for his labour, and if Laban's daughters could have listened at the door, they would have heard the deal they reached. Essentially, their dad told Jacob to name his desired wages, so Jacob did. He didn't request money; instead, he offered to work for Laban for seven years if he could have the hand of the fair Rachel in marriage at the end of that period. Laban had two daughters. Rachel, the younger one, was drop-dead gorgeous, and Leah wasn't. It doesn't take superhuman powers to see who would win that beauty contest, and Jacob was smitten.[159] With underwhelming enthusiasm, Laban agreed, "Well, you may as well have her as anyone else."[160] The plan was in motion.

Before proceeding, we need to address the cultural practice in this scenario. The request for Rachel's hand was purely a business transaction. Jacob didn't have any money to pay a bride price, so he was willing to work seven years in exchange for his heart's desire. In ancient Hebrew

---

[157] Genesis 27:41–45, 28:1–2.

[158] Genesis 29:14.

[159] Genesis 29:15–18.

[160] Genesis 29:19 (paraphrased).

culture, it was the responsibility of the groom or his family to negotiate a financial contract, called a *mohar*, with the bride's father for the privilege of marrying his daughter.[161] It differed from a dowry, in which the bride's family contributed money or property to the marriage.[162] Leah and Rachel didn't have any input into the legal agreement. Their father determined who each daughter would marry and the price the groom would pay. The Western notion of romantic love was not part of the equation. All the warm fuzzies and romance involved in love as we know it were merely a bonus if a couple happened to experience them.

As women of the twenty-first century, we might feel outraged by the injustice of this ancient practice, but women were valued in the Hebrew culture more than this custom alone leads us to believe. Proverbs 31:10–12 says:

> An excellent wife who can find? She is far more precious than jewels. The heart of her husband trusts in her, and he will have no lack of gain. She does him good, and not harm, all the days of her life.

A woman who holds her husband's heart isn't someone of little worth or merely a piece of his property. Proverbs 31 also lists many of the wife's other roles, which are as varied as investing in real estate,[163] caring for the poor and needy,[164] and sewing and selling clothing.[165] These endeavours, and many more mentioned, are far beyond the traditional childbearing and rearing roles or kitchen duties ascribed to women, and they require knowledge, skill, and numerous other qualifications. So we can relax, knowing that women were still esteemed in Leah and Rachel's culture, even though their customs differed from ours.

---

[161] Cohen, ed., *The Jewish Family in Antiquity*, 133.

[162] Meyers, "Dowry," *The Eerdmans Bible Dictionary*, electronic edition, Logos Bible Software.

[163] Proverbs 31:16.

[164] Proverbs 31:20.

[165] Proverbs 31:24.

However, the sisters fit the description of invisible women in my book because they had no control over their lives. Someone else was determining their course, and their futures were nothing more than bargaining chips. Neither Leah nor Rachel was in charge of her own destiny. So let's explore what their futures held.

On Leah's wedding day, all is in readiness. Like many women, I imagine she has dreamed about this day since she was a child and has planned it a hundred times on Pinterest. It's the day she will become Mrs. Jacob. Yes, Leah, not Rachel, will become Mrs. Jacob today. A trick and trade orchestrated by their scheming father will make this a day to remember, but not in the way Leah would hope.

Her soon-to-be husband is responsible and a hard worker. After all, he's been her father's employee for seven years, shown up for work every day, and treated him with respect—at least there are no reported rumours to the contrary. So it's unlikely she has any qualms beyond the usual nervousness any bride experiences about taking that irrevocable step into an unknown future. And similar to wives today, she probably harbours dreams that her uncertain future will become a beautiful life.

As she looks in the mirror, her less-than-gorgeous features, especially compared with her stunning younger sister, reflect back. Her eyes detract from her appearance,[166] which is primarily why she has spent her life in the shadow of the glamorous Miss Middle East, invisible.

Some of us may relate to her plight because we are one of the Leahs of the world. The one left on the sidelines while the Beautiful One in the family seems to enjoy all the advantages. Or possibly, to climb out of the shadows, you become an overachiever to establish your own identity. Your heart breaks when you're the Leah and feel lonely, forgotten, and invisible. Being a Leah *is* hard. Being Leah *was* hard.

But not today. It's the much-dreamed-about day when Leah will become a wife despite her physical shortcomings. As the honoured woman, she will hold her head high as her father presents her to the groom, who will gasp at her transformation and be thrilled with how stunning she looks. In this bride's *happily ever after*, their home will

---

[166] Genesis 29:17.

be a comfortable and secure place where she can bloom as a wife and, eventually, mother. Her culinary prowess will dazzle her doting husband, and she will beautify their humble abode to the best of her ability. For years she has been stitching linens from the highest thread count for her hope chest, and each time her cherished spouse moves in them, they will caress his weathered skin. Nothing will be too much effort for her. At least, that's how I envision her dreams.

The slow ticking of the minutes turns into hours, and at last, the moment arrives. Laban has thrown a big feast for Jacob because he has fulfilled his contract, and the promised wedding is underway.[167] Leah places the veil over her face with trembling hands when her father finally arrives to collect her. Then, leaving her childhood home behind and taking only a collection of memories, she walks toward her husband and into her ever after.

And that is where the fantasy ends because it all implodes. Something terrible happens. The sly Laban substitutes Leah for Rachel, whom he had agreed Jacob would marry. It seems like the plot of a bad movie, with ominous music playing in the background and dim lighting creating shadows. The bride is switched, and the duped groom has no clue until the next morning. It would be hard to believe in a Hallmark movie, and in reality, it seems even harder to believe.

How could it have happened? Whether Jacob was drunk from the big party, or Leah was wearing a veil and her features were unclear in low lighting, a combination of the two, or some other reason, the morning after was a bride's worst nightmare. But unfortunately for Leah, it *did* happen, and the *how* is now lost in the mists of time.

Envisioning what the following morning was like for Leah, I see her awaken and lay still, enjoying her husband's nearness and observing the soft movement of his chest with each breath. Then I see Jacob stir, turn to his darling bride, and utter a giant "AHHHH!" But it's not the "Ahh" of satisfaction as he drinks in the sight of his beloved. Crushing despair overwhelms Leah at her husband's revulsion. Imagine how devastated she feels as her husband bolts from the room, taking part

---

[167] Genesis 29:22.

of her soul with him. The first sounds out of the mouth of her spouse are ones of terror, not adoration. Deserted in her marriage bed, Leah must be in shock, wondering what she's done wrong. Thanks to Dear Old Dad, she's now on the reject pile. Right from the outset. Not the morning after any bride would envision.

Her experience is one of those *before* and *after* incidents that change a life forever. Before it, Leah is invisible because of her sister's beauty and her own lack thereof. Then she has her day in the brilliant sunshine of love. That's precisely what it turns out to be—*one day* in the brilliant sunshine of love. Her husband's rejection steals her short-lived joy and places her squarely in the *after* position, again shrouded in invisibility. At least before her marriage she had the hope of a happy home and a loving husband. Now the after is worse than the before because she is trapped.

The looming question arises: Was Leah complicit in the deception? Sources I consulted generally agreed that Laban was the perpetrator of the fraud. That makes sense from my female point of view because I can't imagine a woman thinking that tricking a man into marrying her—knowing her sister plans to wed him and that he's smitten with the Gorgeous One—could in any way lead to a happy marriage. And believing that she thought the morning revelation would lead to a "Gotcha!" moment and a happily ever after is, I think, in the realm of fantasy and romance novels. It's not likely a woman would believe that she could deceive a man and the result would be that he would love her. It's that simple. It would have been abundantly clear the next morning that the strategy didn't work, and it doesn't take supernatural insight to foresee that outcome. Any woman wants to be loved and cherished, and I don't think she would have been naive enough to think that deliberately stealing her sister's fiancé would achieve that end. She was possibly just as duped by her father as Jacob and Rachel and unwittingly walked into a situation she didn't understand. The trade had tricked them all.

That's all the more reason my heart breaks for Leah. Laban may have told both sisters that Jacob would marry her because it was customary for the elder daughter to marry first. They would have accepted the explanation without question and been unaware of the contract agreed upon by the two men.

Genesis 30:15 also sheds some light on this situation from a later perspective. In the previous verse, Leah's son Reuben finds some mandrakes while harvesting wheat and takes them to his mother. Rachel asks if she may have some of his find. Leah's response is very telling: "*Wasn't it enough that you took away my husband? Will you take my son's mandrakes too?*" (NIV). If Leah had been the one who had stolen Rachel's husband, wouldn't Rachel have accused Leah of taking him rather than the other way around?[168] Her words reveal that Leah considers herself the wronged sister, not Rachel. That supports the position that Leah's motives were pure, and she was not complicit in deceiving Jacob; she honestly thought she was the rightful wife. Laban, the Daddy Dearest of Mesopotamia, completely suckered both daughters.

Then the situation goes from bad to worse for Leah. When Jacob rages to his father-in-law about the grievous deception he has committed, Laban instructs him to finish his honeymoon, and then, if he agrees to work another seven years, he can marry Rachel too.[169] Jacob suffers a gross injustice, but his innocent wife suffers it also.

Can you imagine what a delightful honeymoon that was? A husband merely tolerating his wife because he had to, all the while dreaming of the day he could wed her sister? In the poem "Aedh Wishes for the Cloths of Heaven" by W.B. Yeats, the lover says to his beloved: "I have spread my dreams under your feet; Tread softly because you tread on my dreams."[170]

Lovingly laid before her husband, Leah's dreams were crushed and landed in a tangled heap at her own feet. No one cared enough to tiptoe gently over them—not her husband, and most definitely not her father.

As it turns out, Jacob is an honourable man because he remains married to Leah rather than divorcing her or discarding her like a

....

[168] Farber, "How Is It Possible; Leah Is Not Complicit," para. 3.

[169] Genesis 29:27.

[170] Yeats, "Cloths of Heaven," 60.

pair of old gym shorts. But at the end of the honeymoon week, he acquires Rachel as his second wife. Thus, Jacob becomes the husband of two wives, and no one lives happily ever after. And he has to work for Laban for another seven years as payment for the sought-after Rachel.

Leah has no illusions that she possesses her husband's heart. Forever she is locked in a marriage where her husband's affections rest on another,[171] and she is the invisible wife. But God sees that dejected lady and pursues his Beloved Daughter. Genesis 29:31–32 says:

> When the Lord *saw* that Leah was not loved, he enabled her to conceive, but Rachel remained childless. Leah became pregnant and gave birth to a son. She named him Reuben, for she said, "It is because the Lord has seen my misery. Surely my husband will love me now." (NIV, emphasis added)

Leah may be invisible to her husband, but the Lord sees her. He isn't just aware that she's in an unhappy situation; he *sees* her and responds in a way that helps to soothe the ache in her heart. He allows her to conceive and bear a child to love. The name she chooses for her son, Rueben, reveals that she knows the Lord understands her distress, because it means, *"It is because the Lord has seen my misery."* The name also indicates she realizes she isn't wallowing alone in a fathomless, dark pit, lost forever. She is disconsolate, though, because, above all else, she desires her husband's love. Jacob is her only husband, and looking into a future without his love must seem like a tragic fairy tale in which she plays the lead role. Maybe having another baby will turn the tide.

Apparently not.

The second baby arrives, and she names him Simeon, *"Because the Lord has heard that I am hated, he has given me this son also."*[172] Her

---

[171] Genesis 29:28–30.

[172] Genesis 29:33.

longing for her husband continues as she names her third son Levi, *"Now at last my husband will become attached to me, because I have borne him three sons."*[173] She knows the Lord is on her side, but she longs for a husband who loves and cherishes her for who she is, not just because she's his heir production facility. Although she can't make Jacob love her, God gives her babies to help fill that void in her life. She may be the invisible wife, but she is God's Beloved Daughter.

Next to arrive is Judah: *"This time I will praise the Lord,"*[174] and his name signifies a shift in Leah's attitude. As hard as it may be, there are times when we need to take our attention away from our difficulties and, like Leah, praise the Lord anyway. It isn't something we feel like doing, but it will change our perspective as we exalt the God of the universe who sees us and knows we are struggling. What a journey! Four little ones in the house mean a bustling household, but despite her busyness and emotional distress, she lifts her gaze from her heartbreak and praises the Lord for her family.

Remember how Hannah turned to praise in the middle of her troubles? King David wrote numerous psalms that he began by voicing his anguish, but by the end, he praised God. If we aren't going to stay distressed forever, we must be willing to take a step of faith and shift our focus away from ourselves and onto him. For some of us, wallowing is our natural bent, but we often find the antidote to wallowing is offering praise. Philippians 4:4 says, *"Rejoice in the Lord always; again I will say, rejoice."* In his book *Soul Care*, Rob Reimer says, "There are only two times to worship: when we feel like it, and when we don't. And when we don't feel like it is the time we need it most."[175] Have you noticed that spiritual growth isn't a smooth, straightforward trajectory? Somehow, I think God planned it that way.

For some reason, after her fourth baby, Leah is unable to conceive again. Rachel had given Jacob her servant Bilhah to bear children in her place, so Leah, following her sister's lead, gave her servant Zilpah to her

....

[173] Genesis 29:34.

[174] Genesis 29:35.

[175] Reimer, *Soul Care*, p.196.

husband, who produced two more sons on her behalf.[176] It was a busy family in a different era and culture.

But the time hadn't yet come for Leah to retire to her rocking chair and knit socks while watching old movies. After all those years, she still wanted to win her husband's affection, so she negotiated with her sister for an extra night with hubby. Rachel wanted the mandrakes Leah's son had found for their touted aphrodisiac properties because she struggled with infertility. So they agreed—Rachel got the mandrakes, and Leah got an extra night of marital bliss.[177] Everyone was happy, especially Leah, because she became pregnant.

Do you know why that happened? Because *"God listened to Leah."*[178] After numerous years of striving to win Jacob's love, God understood her desire and still listened. Have you ever prayed for years for something to change and wondered if God even hears you anymore because you've been asking for so long, and nothing seems to change? God still listened to Leah, his Beloved Daughter, so take heart; God is on your side.

Leah pops out three more babies over time, two of whom are boys. The first of these is Issachar, and the next, her last son, is Zebulun, which means *"God has presented me with a precious gift."*[179] Then Leah adds, *"This time my husband will treat me with honor, because I have borne him six sons."*[180] Oh, the longing. After years and years, she still wants to be cherished by her husband, because she continues to feel bereft of his love. Yet repeatedly over those difficult years, God ministers to her. He gives her children to love and raise to serve him, and even though her husband's affections seem out of her reach, she has her family.

Interestingly, Leah's last child was a girl named Dinah, and I think she was a special gift from God.[181] After six boys, I can picture God saying, "Leah, this one's for you!" Boys are an exciting challenge to

---

[176] Genesis 30:9-12.

[177] Genesis 30:15.

[178] Genesis 30:17a.

[179] Genesis 30:20 (NIV).

[180] Genesis 30:20 (NIV).

[181] Genesis 30:21.

raise, as Leah was well aware. My daughter described her elder son as "a ball of noise wrapped in dirt" as a toddler. But girls are something different altogether. Leah took her responsibility of raising her boys seriously, but I think this precious little girl filled a hole in her heart that was pink and fluffy. Dinah brought joy to Leah's life, and God knew she needed it.

Jacob's devotion was absent from Leah's life, and unfortunately, her utter soul-crushing pain was the dark underbelly of the captivating love story between Jacob and Rachel. Despite that, Leah raised some remarkable children. By name, they were: Reuben, Simeon, Levi, Judah, Issachar, Zebulun, and Dinah. From Levi descended Moses and Aaron and the priestly line, the Levites. From Judah descended the royal line, including King David and Jesus. When she named her son Judah, Leah said, "*This time I will praise the Lord,*"[182] and it was from the line of Judah the Messiah was born. Interesting. These were no ordinary children, and she was the mother of them all. What a legacy!

Despite her difficulties, God elevated Leah in a memorable way. She wouldn't fade into the annals of history as an unloved wife whose father tricked her husband into marrying her. No, Leah became the matriarch of a family line that will last for all time—not an invisible woman, but a Beloved Daughter.

Rachel finally marries the man of her dreams. Unfortunately, her older sister had married him first, but we know he loves Rachel dearly, and she basks in that love. The years Jacob spends paying off his debt aren't likely arduous, because he has to work somewhere, and they are together. There is the Leah problem, however. Her presence in Jacob and Rachel's marriage must be a perpetual thorn in the flesh for Rachel, but it's transparent to the world that she is her husband's true love and the one he cherishes.

[182] Genesis 29:35.

And then Leah becomes pregnant, and Rachel watches from the sidelines as her husband steps into his role as a father to the child of his other wife. Patiently, Rachel waits for her turn to surprise Jacob with a grand reveal and tell him they will have a baby. And she waits and waits some more. Leah spawns one child after another, and still, Rachel waits.

Each month ends the same way, with no offspring in the offing, which distresses her and reinforces her feelings of invisibility. Then resentment and jealousy begin to burn in her heart toward her sister. It's easy to understand why she may feel she isn't just a pretty face, arm candy. *She* is the wife Jacob loves—Leah isn't. Yet her rival is the one who produces children so effortlessly it seems as if they come off an assembly line. Eventually, she concludes that her childless state must be Jacob's fault, and she explodes and tells him that if he doesn't give her children, she will die![183] After this outburst, the tension in their home undoubtedly escalates and creates a less-than-delightful atmosphere. Any earlier fantasy she may have had of living in bliss while enveloped in her doting husband's arms disappears like fairy dust.

The parallels between Rachel's life and Hannah's are evident because the other wife in each narrative, though not loved as much, could bear children, while the cherished wife could not. In the chapter on Hannah, we examined the trials she suffered in her home and society, many of which would have been similar for Rachel. There's no evidence in the Bible that Leah mistreated Rachel the way Hannah's co-wife mistreated her; however, when jealousy invades a home, we know relationships are negatively affected. Although Rachel's struggle with invisibility differed from Leah's, she still felt invisible and inferior to her sister, who could fulfill all the roles expected of a wife.

Rather than remain childless, Rachel gives her servant Bilhah to Jacob to act as a surrogate. As a result, Bilhah produces two sons, whom Rachel considers her own and trophies in the competition with her sister.[184] But all is not lost for her on the baby front. Genesis 30:22 says, *"Then God remembered Rachel, and God listened to her ..."* Have you

---

[183] Genesis 30:1.

[184] Genesis 30:2–8.

noticed how often in this tale God sees and remembers these ladies? Repeatedly, I observe that the women who feel invisible in the scriptures are not invisible to God; he pursues them. And like the other invisible women, Rachel too is a Beloved Daughter. Eventually, God "*opened her womb*,"[185] and she bore two natural sons.

We don't need to repeat the discussion on infertility covered in the chapter about Hannah, but if you haven't read it, I encourage you to do so.

Sadly, Rachel died giving birth to her second child. The why rests with God, but we know he loved her and saw her heart. It's critical to note that although she eventually received her dearest wish, children were not a measure of God's love for her. And like Rachel, we are Beloved Daughters because of our relationship with him, and he is in charge of the bigger picture. So take your needs and struggles to him,[186] whatever they may be, and rest in your loving Father's care. You are not invisible to him.

Although Leah and Rachel's marriages began on a difficult note with a trick and a trade, God didn't ignore their distress or favour one sister over the other. He worked things out in his time and his way for both of his Beloved Daughters. You know the expression, "It's not over 'til it's over?" Amid our difficulties, it's often hard to see how everything might work out. The good thing is, we don't have to know. God knows. A situation may not turn out how we anticipate, but there may be a twist coming that we could never have foreseen and that will resolve the issue in a way that makes us look back with wonder and think, *Huh! God did see me. Who would have thought?*

God was in control of Leah and Rachel's lives. They weren't invisible to him, but there were challenges and rough patches along the way for each of them. That's how life is—for all of us—but it doesn't end there.

[185] Genesis 30:22.

[186] Philippians 4:6.

Rachel basked in Jacob's love and ultimately became a mother, which was her all-consuming dream, although, sadly, it was short-lived. Leah treasured her children's affection and took her place forever in history as the ancestor of the priestly line and the Messiah himself.

Their narrative is convoluted and filled with heartache and drama. Nevertheless, it's an account of two invisible women who became Beloved Daughters of a heavenly Father who saw their hearts, pursued them, and gave them help and hope, despite the factors that led to their quagmire. That same God is in control of your life, Beloved Daughter, and even though you may hit challenges and rough patches too, he is not blind to your difficulties and will walk with you and offer help and hope. Reach out; he's there.

8

FROM SCULLERY MAID AND SLACKER TO BELOVED—MARTHA AND MARY

artha and Mary. Two sisters with different priorities, but they both loved Jesus. Martha's kitchen prowess was exemplary, but work was her focus. It took precedence over more valuable pursuits and left her feeling like a scullery maid, lost in the kitchen and invisible. Mary was a lady hidden in the background, quietly learning from Jesus. She wasn't much help with the mundane work needed to run the household though, causing her sister to view her as a slacker.

Time for full disclosure—having been a Martha all my life, I've struggled to understand this story since childhood. I grasp the principle in theory, but practically, the application trips me up every time. Possibly you're wrestling with that quandary too. Or maybe you think Martha was slightly deranged and identify with Mary. Either way, two ladies began as invisible women in this narrative, but their stories don't end there. They each enjoyed a unique relationship with Jesus as his Beloved Daughter.

If you feel unseen and lost in the details of life, delve into their story and see how Jesus' love encompassed both of these sisters, regardless of their personality quirks and flaws. He knows the burdens threatening to overwhelm you, so dig in and learn more about what they discovered and how their lessons can help you.

Mary, Martha, and their brother, Lazarus, lived in Bethany, a town about two miles from Jerusalem. For identification purposes, because there are so many Marys in the Bible, this was Mary of Bethany. The siblings were friends of Jesus; in fact, the scriptures note he loved them and regularly stayed at their house.

Martha was an impeccable hostess; we all know the type. She invites you to her home, not a restaurant where someone else cooks. The food looks like it breezed together of its own free will, and she presents it with flare. Not one item is out of place anywhere in her home. The floors sparkle and the bathroom looks like it's kept for special occasions. Another disclosure—I may be a Martha, but my food doesn't breeze, and my house does not look like it's always ready for a photo shoot.

Comparing their dispositions, Martha was the more outgoing and take-charge sibling of the two, while Mary stayed in the background. Entertaining was Martha's strength because the passage in Luke 10 says she tracked Jesus down when he arrived in their village and invited him to their home before he could make any other plans. Those were not the actions of a reluctant hostess cast in the role with her teeth clenched. If she felt insecure about her housekeeping or cooking, you can be sure someone else would have billeted him.

Feeding guests was Martha's responsibility, and she probably shopped for the food as well as performing the scullery maid duties. Their family dearly loved Jesus, and everyone seemed to enjoy his company when Martha extended the invitation, but it only happened because she made it happen. She did the grunt work. Someone had to feed Jesus, and it didn't happen by magic.

In Bible times, they didn't have kitchen fairies either, and this is where my bias emerges and why I've wrestled with this story. From childhood, my parents taught me that you don't play or do anything enjoyable until you finish your work. My work is never finished as an adult, so I constantly live the shoulds, consistently placing my responsibilities over things like investing more time with friends, reading, or even having fun. If I don't do the work, who will? And that's why Martha's case has always rankled me. However, in studying her story closely, I'm beginning to understand what Jesus was teaching her. So see what you think as you keep reading.

Jesus agrees to stay at the Three Siblings Bed and Breakfast, and after they catch up on everything that's been happening in his world, the initial frenzy begins to dissipate. So he settles in and starts doing what he does best: teach.

The delicious aroma of fresh baking wafts through the house and signals that good things are in store. And then less-than-pleasing sounds begin to emanate from the kitchen as Martha clatters around more than is necessary. She sighs periodically, revealing to everyone present that something is wrong. But whatever her actions, they don't relay her message well enough because, in the end, she has to use her words to make her point.

So what pushes Martha's temper into the danger-of-exploding zone? According to Luke 10:40, Mary just sits there, listening to Jesus, and doesn't do anything to help with the tasks calling for attention. First, there's lunch to make, and after cleaning up from that meal, she must start preparations for the next. People need to eat, and that means someone has to prepare it.

Perhaps there had previously been friction between the two sisters concerning this issue. In families, children often wiggle out of the chores they hate and gravitate toward the ones they dislike the least. I suspect a history between these siblings led to Martha's complaint because a single incident wasn't likely to aggravate her to the same degree. Mom was no longer around, so there was no matriarch to prod Mary into action or to mediate the dispute. The Scullery Maid and the Slacker were at odds.

From the priority Martha gives to her kitchen duties, we see that serving Jesus is her love language, her way of expressing love. However, doing it alone isn't in her plan, and her irritation finally bubbles over. Being the forthright person she is, she plunks her complaint squarely before Jesus that her sister is being lazy and leaving her with all the work. She demands that he insists that Mary do something and stop just sitting around.[187]

Jesus must have been a close friend because I can't imagine griping to my guest that I was working on his behalf while my sister was lounging. But that's what Martha did. Definitely a cringy move. Her testiness, I think, was Martha's way of telling Jesus she felt invisible. *Here I am, working all by myself, Jesus, and no one is helping or noticing. I'm invisible.*

Being the one stuck in the kitchen all the time, even though you enjoy cooking, isn't always fun. Sometimes you'd like to be the one sitting at the grown-up table rather than getting dish-pan hands. If Jesus had told Mary to help her sister, I suspect Martha would have felt heard, her worth validated, and her contribution appreciated.

His response to Martha's grievance, however, is somewhat unexpected. Instead of playing the Daddy role, telling Mary to vacate her cozy armchair and assist her sister, he directs Martha's focus to the importance of Mary's choice. Calmly, he looks at her stressed face and says, *"Martha, Martha, you are anxious and troubled about many things, but one thing is necessary. Mary has chosen the good portion, which will not be taken away from her."*[188]

Do you relate to her indignation? There she is, feeling like the victim in this situation, and Jesus reprimands *her*, not Mary. He does so kindly, but it's a reprimand nonetheless. He admonishes the person slogging away in the kitchen and says the slacker made the better choice. I know. That isn't our intuitive response, except Jesus works from a different perspective. He doesn't tell Mary to get into the kitchen; he encourages both women to get *out* of the kitchen. Not words a woman usually hears from a man, but they reveal his heart. He sees Martha. She isn't invisible

---

[187] Luke 10:40.

[188] Luke 10:41–42.

to him. Rather than dismiss her concerns, he acknowledges that she's stressed with all her responsibilities and then digs deeper to redirect her attention.

Why did Jesus defend Mary and gently reproach Martha? Remember, he had limited time to disciple people during his earthly ministry. His mission was to teach his followers and impact their lives as much as he could before his death. There wasn't much time to get distracted by the minutia of life. Mary was absorbing all she could, while Martha was preoccupied with the mundane chores of life, the clutter that so easily robs us of the best. Mary got it, and Martha missed it. Whether Jesus ate a homemade lasagna or a frozen one from a supermarket was irrelevant. The latter choice would have offended the seasoned hostess, but clearly not Jesus. He wanted Martha's time, not her service. Being willing to set aside her ideals of hospitality—or even her need to display her abundant talents in that area—to focus on the Lord would require an epic shift in Martha's mindset and, perhaps, a difficult one.

One of the most enjoyable evenings I can remember occurred decades ago when some retired missionaries invited me to their home for a snack of tea and toast. If they asked you over for lunch or dinner, hot dogs were the delicacy they served. Over time, many people enjoyed their hospitality, and whether it was a meal or a snack, it tasted like the food of the gods. They shared it with the joy and love of Jesus that flowed from them, and when he is present, nothing else matters. The food is purely functional. The presence of Jesus in a home is the element that touches lives.

That was the lesson Jesus was trying to impress upon Martha, who felt invisible and overwhelmed. *I'm important—the chores are not. So make simple choices and join Mary at my feet.* When Jesus was gone, Martha would remember what Jesus had taught more than the beef Wellington she served him, which took two days to prepare.

Time passes, and Jesus carries on his ministry in other communities. And then one day, Lazarus becomes seriously ill. Martha and Mary send Jesus a message that they urgently need him, and he replies that they shouldn't worry because "*this illness does not lead to death. It is for the glory of God, so that the Son of God may be glorified through it.*"[189] And so they wait, and wait, and wait. He doesn't come immediately, and the sisters' distress increases as they watch Lazarus's condition deteriorate with every passing minute. They've done everything in their power to help their brother, but before Jesus arrives, the inconceivable happens. Lazarus dies.[190]

It's evident from the account of his death that Martha is frustrated because Jesus hadn't bounded into town when they first summoned him. When he appears four days later, which to the sisters must have felt like an eternity, she is not happy. Really not happy. While Mary remains at home, Martha runs to meet Jesus,[191] both women assuming their usual roles. I can almost envision steam pouring from her ears when she faces Jesus. The accusation that tumbles out reveals her hurt at his seeming lack of concern. Had he come when they summoned him, he could have healed Lazarus and prevented this terrible thing.[192] The invisible lady, relegated to the kitchen, must again have felt invisible because Jesus, whom she loves and who she thought loved their family in return, had ignored their urgent plea. In her distress, she is unaware that he has travelled to reach them at significant personal risk because, as the disciples had cautioned, the Jews wanted to stone him, so it wasn't safe.[193] The threat of imminent death doesn't appear to worry him because he comes anyway and encounters Martha's displeasure for his trouble.

It's hard to believe someone on the periphery of his life would dare to speak to Jesus the way Martha did, so he must have been a dear friend. Hidden in her harsh words, though, was a subtle statement of faith. She acknowledged that Jesus had the power to heal Lazarus, but she was upset because he missed the chance to fix things as she thought they should be fixed—her way. After all, Lazarus had died four days previously because Jesus had taken his sweet time getting there.

....

[189] John 11:4.

[190] John 11:11–13.

[191] John 11:20.

[192] John 11:21.

[193] John 11:8.

When you're the Son of God, you can work on whatever schedule you please because you're the Son of God. It didn't matter to Jesus if Lazarus had been dead for a day, a month, or a decade. We benefit from hindsight, knowing that Jesus knew that Lazarus's death was temporary and that he had a plan to glorify God through it.[194] We've read the end of the story. But the sisters didn't have that advantage. They only heard that Lazarus's illness wouldn't lead to death, and now their brother was dead. Reconciling Jesus' words with reality would have been a challenge.

Despite Martha's complaint, her next statement reveals the depth of her faith in Jesus: "*But even now I know that whatever you ask from God, God will give you.*"[195] Her manner may be gruff, and she expresses her grief by finding fault with Jesus' handling of the situation, but at the core of her being, she has an unshakable faith in her teacher. That is spiritual growth. To her credit, she hasn't squandered the opportunity she had to learn from the master.

Jesus doesn't choose that moment to give Martha an attitude adjustment and set her straight about precisely whom she is accusing of being late. Gently, he gazes at her and tells her everything will be all right, that Lazarus will rise again. He sees her. Evidently, his past teaching had stayed with her because she missed his statement's literal meaning that her brother would come to life again. She agrees that Lazarus will "*rise again in the resurrection on the last day,*"[196] something he has taught her, which will ultimately happen after death. In response, Jesus offers Words of Life to her and to all who follow. If she doesn't yet understand that he is the Messiah, all doubt leaves her when he says, "*I am the resurrection and the life. Whoever believes in me, though he die, yet shall he live, and everyone who lives and believes in me shall never die.*"[197] After that proclamation, he asks Martha—the sister who first chose service over devotion, the invisible woman lost in the kitchen—if she believes it. And then she crosses into the position of Beloved Daughter as she

[194] John 11:4.

[195] John 11:22.

[196] John 11:24.

[197] John 11:25–26.

stands, squares her shoulders, and replies, "*Yes, Lord; I believe that you are the Christ, the Son of God, who is coming into the world.*"[198] These words change her life, "*Yes, Lord, I believe.*"

I have said those words. I have chosen to believe and accept the gift Jesus offered and follow him. His death on the cross sealed my eternal position when he took my sins and paid the penalty for me. With those words, I became a Beloved Daughter. If you haven't taken that step and would like to become a follower of Jesus and enter into a relationship as God's Daughter, I encourage you to do so. At the back of this book is a section titled "How to Become a Follower of Christ," and it can help you on your journey.

Jesus did deal with the Lazarus issue, but we'll explore Mary's role before we delve into how he did so.

What about Mary? She was the quiet, sensitive soul in the family. Her comfort zone was in the background, which made her largely invisible to the world. In comparison, her sister was the public face of their family, a more forceful person and a little prickly. And Mary lived in her shadow. Martha was like the General Manager of the Universe and could find more jobs than a servant polishing silver at Buckingham Palace. The kitchen was her domain, and she always saw something that needed doing, with no end in sight. When Mary helped with the chores, she was probably the extra hands to do the job, not the team leader. Hot dogs would have been a Mary kind of meal, served in a relaxed setting with friends, but Martha had higher standards, hence the tension. Remember the hostess extraordinaire we discussed earlier? That wasn't Mary, definitely not her calling.

When Jesus visits, we glimpse Mary's personality from her interactions with him more than from her words because her words are few. The opportunity to listen and learn as she sits at the teacher's feet is a

---

[198] John 11:27.

privilege Mary fully embraces. Jesus takes the time to teach her and doesn't discount this eager student because of her gender; she's not invisible to him. Many men would have taken their place soaking in his teachings, but it delights me that scripture paints this picture of a woman as a learner. Jesus encourages her to adopt that role over assuming that of a servant. Studying at the Bethany Rabbinical School isn't even a remote possibility for her, but what a treat she enjoys—a private audience with the master, a seminary like no other.

Not only is Mary enjoying a forum granted few, but she also receives Jesus' blessing. He affirms her and expresses his approval when he says, *"Mary has chosen the good portion, which will not be taken away from her."*[199] How remarkable is that? He doesn't let her sister harass her into missing such a rare opportunity, and he values the role of learner so much that he encourages her to be a slacker. How often does that happen? Mary may be invisible to the world around her and an enigma to her sister, but to Jesus, she's a Beloved Daughter who sits at his feet and absorbs every lesson she can.

When Lazarus dies, the curtain that hides the quiet Mary parts again, and we glimpse her sensitive nature. John 11:28–36 describes this drama. While Mary waits with the group of mourners in their home, Martha runs to meet Jesus on the outskirts of town. When he arrives, he doesn't bolt into the community and immediately locate the deceased Lazarus to perform his miracle but sends Martha back to fetch her sister. Mary is also a Beloved Daughter, not an invisible woman. And thankfully, he doesn't treat her as unimportant, leaving her to hear about his marvellous feat later.

Out the door faster than a crowd disperses when a performer passes a hat to collect money, she scrambles off to meet Jesus. When she arrives, hair flying and chest heaving, she drops at his feet, sobbing, and gives full vent to her emotions. As she openly weeps in front of Jesus, the comforters who follow her also weep,[200] undoubtedly triggered by her manifestation of grief. How dearly she loved her brother is evident to all,

---

[199] Luke 10:42b.

[200] John 11:29, 33.

and she doesn't try to hide it from Jesus or the crowd. Martha's crusty exterior hides her emotions, but Mary expresses hers and, in so doing, exposes her vulnerability. Eventually her feelings find words and tumble out: "*Lord, if you had been here, my brother would not have died.*"[201]

Mary's grief emerges as a complaint, but like Martha, the complaint reveals her faith. It shows that she knows Jesus is no ordinary rabbi and that he has the power to heal. The heartbreak and devastation she feels, writ large all over her, are not a mystery to anyone as she lays her burden before him. Pretending she doesn't feel like her insides have been ripped out and torn to shreds isn't an option. Her sorrow and the depth of her pain are laid bare before him.

Jesus doesn't dismiss the sea of grief surrounding him by trying to jolly everyone along or asking them to stop the noise because everything will work out in the end. Instead, their dearly-loved teacher does something that tells us as much about himself as it does about his love for these sisters. He weeps.[202] Jesus loves these women so much that he profoundly feels their grief; their pain is not invisible to him. And he also loved Lazarus.

When Jesus arrives at the cave where the body is buried, he is deeply moved a second time. Not a disinterested bystander or gawker, Jesus participates fully in the mourning process. In the Sermon on the Mount, he says, "*Blessed are those who mourn, for they shall be comforted.*"[203] This teacher understands Mary and Martha's grief first-hand, and their expression of it reaches his heart.[204]

But there is good news coming. Lazarus's death isn't permanent, as the women fear. Jesus brings him back to life sensationally after he's been dead for four days. Martha is concerned that her brother won't smell like roses after that length of time, but Jesus doesn't show any distress. If he can raise a four-day-old body from the dead, he can deodorize it somewhere along its route to life. Jesus asks them (presumably the group

....

[201] John 11:32.

[202] John 11:35.

[203] Matthew 5:4.

[204] John 11:33–36.

of mourners accompanying the women) to move the stone away from the mouth of the burial cave, and then he commands Lazarus to come out. And Lazarus does.[205] The former corpse resembles a mummy when he steps out of the tomb into the fresh country air, with his hands and feet bound with burial cloths and another over his face, and no parfum de dead body emanates from him. Now that's a dramatic entrance and testament to the power of God. Equally dramatic is the love it expresses to the two Beloved Daughters.

This miraculous raising of Lazarus leads to Mary's subsequent moving demonstration of love and devotion to Jesus. Sometime later, he's again visiting the home of the three siblings. True to form, Martha is hostessing and serving dinner while the rejuvenated Lazarus relaxes at the table with the Lord. Mary's contribution is entirely different. She enters the dining room, not presenting a gourmet delicacy but bearing a little box of expensive perfume worth a year's wages. Sitting before her is the one who loves her so much that he brought her brother back to life. Words could never communicate the depth of love for Jesus that Mary's next act conveys.[206]

That Beloved Daughter kneels before her Lord and gently takes his foot in her hands. She opens her prized box of perfume, and the aroma that wafts out delights the senses of each person present. It isn't a bottle of discount-store cologne that any teenager could produce. The gift she offers is her most treasured possession, and it's not an impulsive act. Thoughtfully, she has pondered her idea and then, fully aware of the decision she's making, gives an incomparable gift to the man who will become the Saviour of the world.

Cradling Jesus' foot, she gently massages it with the scented ointment. Then she grasps his other foot and repeats her careful application. The fragrance intensifies in the room as she works, and it's so exotic I wonder if any of the people present would have ever had an experience to equal it. But her ministrations don't end there. Mary doesn't use an old towel or even a guest towel to finish her task. Completely absorbed in her

---

[205] John 11:41–44.

[206] John 12:1–3.

work, this humble lady lowers her head, takes her long, silky hair, and tenderly wipes her master's feet.[207]

That exquisite gift Mary gave Jesus was an investment of love, not from an invisible woman, but from a Beloved Daughter. Do you get chills as I do just imagining what that experience was like for her? I wish I could have done that for him, but would I have?

Judas, the disciple of Jesus who later betrayed him, and who was the keeper of their finances, strongly disapproves of Mary's action. He grumbles that she should have given the money to the poor.[208] Right. That comes from a thief who enjoys his position as the treasurer because he can pilfer the coffers at will. A donation of that amount would be a tidy sum to allegedly disburse under the guise of charity while padding his retirement fund. Jesus, however, sees Mary's tribute in a different light. He accepts her extraordinary gift as an expression of love, not a foolish extravagance, because he adamantly commands Judas to leave the lady alone. Nor is there any false modesty on his part. He accepts Mary's worship in the way she chooses to bestow it and gives her permission to use the remaining perfume at his burial rather than pressuring her, Judas-style, to gift it to the poor.[209] Martha hadn't been allowed to rob Mary of the opportunity to learn from Jesus, and Jesus doesn't allow Judas, through misplaced obligation, to rob Mary of the offering she will bring to his burial either.

Mary could have derailed her plan had she worried about how others would perceive and judge her gift. But thankfully, she didn't overthink it or allow fear to steal the experience of a lifetime from her. There are two lessons here for me—to keep my focus on Jesus and not be concerned with what others may think about how I serve him and to allow others to worship in their own way without my judgement about how they do it. What joy would have been lost for Mary and Jesus had she succumbed to the pressure of living up to someone else's misguided expectations.

....

[207] John 12:3.

[208] John 12:4–6.

[209] John 12:7–8.

Mary wasn't an invisible woman. She was a Beloved Daughter, and Jesus approved of her and her choices. In the Parable of the Bags of Gold, the master said to his servant, "*Well done, good and faithful servant … Enter into the joy of your master.*"[210] I see those words in Mary's future and want to live my life to be worthy of them.

Martha, who felt like a scullery maid unseen in the kitchen, struggled to be noticed and to have her contribution appreciated. Jesus didn't judge her for her short-sightedness but pursued her and redirected her gaze from mundane, everyday concerns to the eternal realm and the importance of spending time with him. The Words of Life he offered her changed her destiny and have brought life to generations of followers of Christ. Jesus saw Martha and loved her, prickles and all, his Beloved Daughter.

If you think the takeaway from Jesus' endorsement of Mary is licence to skip the dishes and leave them to someone else because spiritual people don't dirty their hands with the grunge work of life, think again. Wrong message. God would rather we give him our hearts than our money, service to others, or sacrifices of any kind. All those things are valuable (like helping with the dishes), and we shouldn't neglect them; however, he wants more—our core. Our service flows from our relationship with him, not as a replacement for it.

Even though she appeared to be a slacker, Mary had the right idea. She basked in Jesus' presence when she could and blessed him with her precious gift. With her quiet personality, she is hidden in the background, seemingly unnoticed. But Jesus pursued this gentle lady. He protected her from the impositions of others and encouraged her to grow in her faith. Mary's heart belonged to her Lord, and we understand the depth of her love through her actions. And like Martha, Mary wasn't invisible either.

---

[210] Matthew 25:21.

The sisters' identities were much more than the scullery maid and the slacker. That's where their stories began, but Beloved Daughters is who they were—a distinction worth pondering.

Like these ladies, God knows your burdens, loves you, and encourages you to spend time in his presence. His heart longs to connect with your heart. If you haven't joined the family of God, he's waiting with open arms to welcome you. *"For great is his steadfast love toward us, and the faithfulness of the Lord endures forever ..."* (Psalm 117:2).

From Imperfect to Beloved—
The Woman at the Well and the
Adulterous Woman

an you think of a person whose name you immediately link with something inappropriate, or worse, that she has done? Do you know anything else about her, such as her interests, accomplishments, or positive character traits? Unfortunately, one poor decision, or a series of them, and the associated stigma can overshadow any merits and render one's virtues invisible. This is especially true with today's ready access to social media. Not a situation anyone would desire, and a plight that can be difficult to escape.

That problem isn't limited to our times.—we can read about it in the Bible. The stories contained in scripture aren't about perfect people. Some of them had a long way to go to move the needle on the meter in the perfection direction. That might astound you if you're unfamiliar with this ancient work, but they were real women with real problems, failings, and even outright sins—anything but perfect, just like you and me.

In the book of John, two women made choices that placed them squarely in the imperfect category. Their decisions caused them to be labelled and judged, entrapping them in a mire that—while of their own making—threatened to ruin their lives forever. They started as sinners like the rest of us; however, their sins were a little more visible because people knew how they had transgressed. Their virtues were invisible—what they had done was not. As a result, one woman's community despised her, and the other's sin qualified her for death row. Until Jesus came, that is. He saw these women, not just their sins, and after their encounters with him, they walked away from his presence as Beloved Daughters—changed.

Let's explore how Jesus freed these ladies from their burden of guilt and shame and how he can do the same for us.

Jesus was travelling one day and stopped for a rest and a drink at Jacob's Well Refreshment Centre while his disciples hustled off to buy food. Actually, it was Jacob's Well, a historic communal well that the locals frequented in Samaria, which lay between two Jewish territories. To say the Samaritans and Jews weren't friendly with each other would be an understatement, so his stop there is noteworthy. Weary from ministering and his travels, he took a break and waited for lunch to arrive. It was about noon, the hottest part of the day, so there weren't many people fetching water.[211]

Enter the lady of the hour, a Samaritan. Muscling an oversized stone crock, she arrives at the well to collect the water she needs to meet the demands of her day. This action indicates her social class because she comes to draw the water by herself rather than sending a servant. It's heavy grunt work, the type that women worldwide perform for their families. Some haul water, some haul bags of grain, and some haul groceries. They all lug them home. This lady doesn't drive up in a BMW,

---

[211] John 4:1–6.

fill her giant water jugs, and throw them in the trunk. Whatever she loads, she has to carry. And water is heavy. It's also sweltering on this day, making her task all the more unpleasant.

Why would she choose to do this work at noon? It's not as if it's a surprise that she needs water. Why not wait for the cool of the evening, or get it done early in the morning before the temperature hits scorching, as mothers in every culture teach their children to do? The reason becomes clear as her conversation with Jesus unfolds.

While he rests his aching feet by the well, the sun beating on his head, the lady approaches. He asks if she could give him a drink.[212] This tired man doesn't have a cup, bucket, or any implement to draw water himself. He isn't following the Boy Scout motto, "Be Prepared," but that's probably by design—his pursuit of this particular lady, and she will ultimately benefit from his decision.

His simple request astonishes the woman, and she questions why on earth he would ask her for a drink. She's a Samaritan and knows the Jews have nothing to do with Samaritans.[213] Already she identifies herself as an invisible woman because she's from the wrong gene pool, a group of people the Jews consider inferior. Not only that, but Jesus is a man, speaking with her, a woman, and it appears they are alone, which is not accepted in her society either. She determines from some clue, possibly his accent and dress, that he's a Jew, making her well aware that he's crossing lines and violating social rules just by engaging her in conversation. He continues the dialogue and gives a puzzling response to her question, "*If you knew the gift of God, and who it is that is saying to you, 'Give me a drink,' you would have asked him, and he would have given you living water.*"[214] First, he asks her for a drink, which is against all the rules, and then he speaks in riddles. Who is this man?

Have you ever felt like Jesus was speaking to you in riddles? Much like this confused lady, we might only see part of the picture and have to trust that he knows more than we do. His new acquaintance points

[212] John 4:7–8.

[213] John 4:9.

[214] John 4:10.

out that the well is deep, and Jesus doesn't have a container to draw water. How is he even going to get the living water? Obstacles. She sees obstacles, just like I do. Every time. *God, that can't happen because.* She doesn't ask, but I'm sure she wonders, *What is he talking about? Living water? What's that?* And her next question implies, *Who do you think you are anyway?* What she voices is, *"Are you greater than our father Jacob? He gave us the well and drank from it himself, as did his sons and his livestock."*[215] Between the lines, I read her implied thought, *The nerve!*

Jesus doesn't turn and walk away with the attitude *I gave you your chance,* leaving her to continue her invisible existence. Instead, he uses her question to pique her interest further and continue the conversation. Yet again, in riddles, Jesus delivers a sales pitch to her, extolling the virtues of his living water. Setting it up, he explains that anyone who drinks ordinary well water will ultimately become thirsty again. Of course. That's basic life knowledge. But he has something better to offer—way better. His marvellous water has benefits she can only dream possible; she will never be thirsty again if she drinks it. To her, that means she will never feel the discomfort of thirst again, and bonus, she'll be released from the drudgery of her miserable daily chore. The lady is ecstatic! No more trips to the well. No more hauling water, day after day, in the rain, in the sleet, in the snow. Then Jesus tells her the best part of what's probably starting to sound like a magic potion. Once consumed, the water will transform itself inside her to become *"an artesian spring … gushing fountains of endless life."*[216] She is enthralled! Her response? "Please, sir, give me that totally awesome stuff so I won't have to keep coming back here!"[217]

And then Jesus drills into the heart of the matter: who this woman is, and what she genuinely needs. He says, "Okay. Go and get your husband and then come back."[218] But the lady doesn't have a husband. When she admits as much, he commends her for being honest and then

[215] John 4:12.

[216] John 4:14 (MSG).

[217] John 4:15 (paraphrased).

[218] John 4:16 (paraphrased).

reveals that he already knows all about her marital status. Adding to the mystery of who he is, Jesus mentions that the partner with whom she now cohabits is not her husband, and buried in her past lay five ex-husbands.[219] That's not usually information tossed into a conversation when you first meet someone, especially so early in the discussion. However, Jesus isn't one to adhere to social rules for politeness' sake when he has a deeper agenda.

Now we understand why this woman is drawing water in the middle of the day. There doesn't seem to be any other water traffic, so she's chosen to travel to the well during off-peak hours when others are at home enjoying lunch and a siesta. It's quite likely she's not the most popular person in her neighbourhood—not with the women, anyway. She has had five ex-husbands, and now another man is living with her. We have no idea what family carnage lies in the wake of her former lovers' pasts, but heartbreak undoubtedly litters at least some of them. In North American society today, if you've been married and divorced five times, you're as likely to be a celebrity as a social pariah. Not then. She would have been all too aware that her community didn't readily accept her lifestyle. So by avoiding busy times at the community gathering place, she didn't need to speak with anyone, nor did they need to chat with her. Invisibility seems prudent in that light.

Some issues in this woman's life must have caused her to make those choices, but sadly, it seems she lived on the fringes of society. She may not have had a solid support group to help her work through problems, and with each subsequent marriage and divorce, her reputation worsened, and possibly her social circle dwindled with it. Not a spiral one would desire. She didn't even marry her most recent beau, and whether that was her choice or his, we don't know, but we know her life was unstable.

Isn't it extraordinary that Jesus chose to pursue that woman and liberate her from the trap of her own poor choices? He didn't select someone who just needed a little tweaking here or there. She was an honest-to-goodness-fixer-upper woman! So many of us try to appear as if we only require a little tweak when we need a complete inner

---

[219] John 4:17–18.

renovation. Let's see how Jesus transformed that despised woman into a Beloved Daughter.

As it turns out, our lady friend is quite astute, and she tells Jesus she perceives he is a prophet.[220] She isn't alarmed by him or what he says about her, and she doesn't ask what magic he used to uncover her secrets. Her intuitive conclusion is that he's a prophet. A prophet speaks for God, so not a bad deduction. But he's so much more than that, which he soon reveals to her.

The next words out of her mouth make me laugh because they reveal that she's so much like me. A man, who she perceives as a prophet, is sitting in front of her. Rather than being awed by God's power operating in him, she deflects the focus away from herself and her obvious personal issues and asks him to clarify a point of religious practice. My pastor once joked that when he gets to heaven, he wants to ask God what he was thinking when he made kale. Human nature tends to drag us away from the important and focus on the inconsequential.

When you've been raised in a religious tradition, and someone you perceive as an authority on the subject enters the scene, wouldn't it be logical to ask him your faith-related question? That was her approach. Wouldn't it be even better if you were on the winning side of the debate, which I'm sure was her hope? What an opportunity she almost lost to tap into the power of God. When I think of the time that I, and others with me, have spent discussing minor points of scripture when we could have earnestly sought to know the heart of God, I cringe—such a human thing to do.

Jesus takes the time to answer her question about who is worshipping correctly, but he uses his answer to redirect her to the truth he wants her to grasp. He responds that *where* one worships ultimately won't matter, but *how* one worships will. God seeks someone who will "*worship the Father in Spirit and truth.*"[221] Jesus doesn't create an enormous list of shoulds for her to follow to worship rightly. Her relationship with God is his concern, not all the peripheral distractions. Freeing her to worship

....

[220] John 4:19.

[221] John 4:23–24.

God is his purpose, not setting up a new regimen of rules for her to obey that will project her right back into the mire of worshipping from obligation, not love. Sometimes I think we as a church and followers of Christ get a little foggy on that distinction. Worth considering, for me also.

Then her words open the door to a life-altering experience, "*I know that Messiah is coming (he who is called Christ). When he comes, he will tell us all things.*"[222] She's just told the Son of God that she's waiting for him, but she has no idea he's the person sitting before her. It doesn't even enter her consciousness that he is indeed the Messiah. At that moment, Jesus lifts the fog clouding her understanding and reveals his true identity.

Can you fathom how she felt when Jesus responded, "*I who speak to you am he*"?[223] That was a goose-bump-worthy pronouncement. In my mind, I see her jaw drop, her eyes pop wide open, and I hear her gasp as if someone punched her in the abdomen. How could it be? The Messiah she'd been waiting for her entire life was there with her at the well. Her! An insignificant person whom polite society had relegated to the background—discounted because she was unworthy of their company, invisible—was *the* one Jesus pursued and to whom he chose to reveal himself, welcoming her as a Beloved Daughter.

The disciples are dumbfounded when they return from their shopping expedition to find Jesus in deep conversation with a woman. But to their credit, they refrain from speaking and neither ask stupid questions nor intrude on this God-moment.[224]

After concluding the discussion, our leading lady abandons her water jar, because water is the last thing on her mind when she learns she's been casually conversing with the Messiah. She speeds into town as if her hair were on fire. Then, panting, words tumbling out of her mouth almost faster than her mind can form them, she announces, "You have to come! You won't believe it! This guy just told me everything I've

---

[222] John 4:25.

[223] John 4:26.

[224] John 4:27.

ever done! Can he be the Messiah?"[225] She's more frenzied than if she'd witnessed a fifty-donkey pile-up on the highway to Galilee.

The outcome? The people go with her to see this Messiah. In itself, that's striking. She lived her life on the periphery of her community, but this is epic news, and she's willing to risk them thinking she's hallucinating. The chains of her invisibility break apart at that moment as she shares her world-shattering experience. *Jesus has come!*

Do you know what the impact of that lady's action was? Masses of Samaritan people from that town put their faith in Jesus. All because she used her voice to declare to anyone who would listen what he had done.[226] She didn't wander home, pleased that he'd spoken with her, a woman of little account, and then quietly savour the cherished memory of that unforgettable day for the rest of her life. Instead, she let the world know what he'd done so they also could meet Jesus.

That group of new believers asks Jesus if he will please come and stay with them, and he says, "Sure."[227] He is a Jew; had he been any other Jew, he probably would have felt as if they'd asked him to go slumming. Not Jesus. Social rules don't even make it to the bottom of his list of concerns, especially when reaching people with his message is his priority—people of any nationality. And then even more people believe in him when they hear his words.[228]

The Samaritan woman's hair wasn't really on fire when she ran to enlighten the townspeople. But she certainly ignited a spark that paid off eternally for many of her neighbours. They didn't believe because of what she told them; they believed because they met Jesus and recognized that he was genuine. They told her so.[229] No longer a despised, invisible woman, she was a Beloved Daughter who helped bring many people to faith along with her. She wasn't someone who thought she was good enough, had done enough, or would eventually acquire enough brownie

....

[225] John 4:29 (paraphrased).

[226] John 4:39.

[227] John 4:40 (paraphrased).

[228] John 4:41.

[229] John 4:42.

points to cross the divide between herself and God. She knew she needed a Saviour. I don't think Jesus chose her by accident. Do you?

The book of John relates another story of a woman who enters in a less-than-commendable manner.[230] The week-long Feast of Booths, or The Feast of Tabernacles, was in full swing in Jerusalem. It was "celebrated at the time of the agricultural harvest, in gratitude for [God's] present and historical provision."[231] For the event, people stayed in little shelters or booths they built from tree branches, as instructed in Leviticus 23:39–43. The purpose of living in these rough structures was so "[their descendants] *may know that I* [God] *made the people of Israel dwell in booths when I brought them out of the land of Egypt.*"[232] It was a festive occasion of thanksgiving and remembrance of their time spent in the wilderness.[233]

The misbehaving woman in the hot spot attended the feast, but her party abruptly ended when she was hauled from her shack, presumably kicking and screaming. It probably wasn't how she would have planned to end her festivities. A rickety hut made of tree branches, with a life expectancy of one week, wasn't likely soundproof. That might explain how she was caught doing what she shouldn't have been doing. Congested neighbourhoods don't offer much privacy at the best of times, so a campground full of forts would have made her even more vulnerable to discovery. And discovered she was. Committing adultery.

Until that moment, we don't know anything about this woman's life. Since she doesn't come with a sordid backstory dogging her, she may have lived a quiet and ordinary life, invisible to all but her immediate

---

[230] John 8:1–10.

[231] Austin, "Booths, Feast of," *The Lexham Bible Dictionary,* electronic ed.

[232] Leviticus 23:43.

[233] Zimmerman, "Sukkot, The Feast of Booths (Known to Some as the Feast of Tabernacles)," par. 1–2.

contacts. Or her reputation might have preceded her, which led to her capture in compromising circumstances. We do know that from the moment she was arrested for the crime of adultery, who she was—her dreams, aspirations, and even any worthy contributions to society— became invisible, entirely obscured by what she had done. Unfortunately for her, it was the morality police of the time, the religious leaders known as the scribes and Pharisees, who captured her.[234] The penalty for the sin of adultery was as severe as it gets—death,[235] and there was no way out of her predicament, because she couldn't deny her guilt. However, happily, her captors dragged her to Jesus to adjudicate her case rather than some other religious authority.

Before we look closely at her situation and Jesus' response, I want to clarify that the purpose of this story is not to diminish or discount her sin. Jesus didn't diminish or discount any sin in scripture. He treated all sin as sin but loved the people who committed it. He still does. John 3:17 says, *"For God did not send his Son into the world to condemn the world, but in order that the world might be saved through him."* The point of the story is to show God's love and mercy, not that breaking his law didn't matter. It did. But Jesus' intent was more profound than meting out punishment. That makes this story all the more meaningful. The accused lady had committed a serious offence, but Jesus could see past the infraction to the suffering woman standing before him.

Trembling before some powerful religious leaders, this terrified woman's disgrace is exposed for all to see. Guilty as charged. Hmm. It requires two people to commit the criminal act of adultery. So why is only one person being held accountable, especially since death is the penalty for *both* guilty parties? Possibly her partner in crime escaped before they could seize him. Who knows? But the crucial point is that the story focuses on how Jesus rescues her, a woman in deep trouble.

The morality police don't need to produce a written copy of the law to convince her of her misconduct. She knows she is guilty. How could she refute the evidence against her? Placing myself in her situation, I see

....

[234] John 8:3.

[235] Deuteronomy 22:22; Leviticus 20:10.

the "should haves" flood her like a tsunami, and her mind screaming, *Idiot! How could you have been so stupid? What was I thinking?* Now she has to pay the price.

Sometimes one wrong decision carries lifelong consequences, which can be overwhelming when one realizes its full impact. The guilty lady has committed no small misdemeanour that will blow over in a day or two, and she's under no illusion that it will. She is doomed. Her prosecutors even remind Jesus that the Law of Moses states death is the penalty for such a transgression.[236] A cold sweat envelops her as she stands, shaking, before Jesus, because he can decree whether she lives or dies.

The captured woman may not know that the pious men have singled her out as a pawn in a game to trap Jesus so they can arrest him. Her own poor choice has left her vulnerable. The situation is more about Jesus than her, but she's caught between the two sides. The Jews have been trying to find grounds to arrest this man who is a disturber, and they want him stopped. He's been interfering with their neat and tidy religious traditions and beliefs for too long, and it needs to end.

So there she stands, invisible as a person, merely a sinner—and a test case for Jesus. Not a test to determine if the law is valid, but to see if Jesus will uphold the law and punish her. What will he do? Will this be the day she dies, only to be buried dishonourably in an unmarked plot, or worse, in a grave with her disgrace etched on the stone, eternally linking her name and her shame?

Jesus is aware of her plight. He sees the frightened woman, her dishevelled appearance, and, most of all, her need for a rescuer. Not a rescuer to extract her from a situation she helped create, but a rescuer who will forgive her. Sin doesn't just disappear; it pokes its head up somewhere else in time and can become an intolerable weight, so ignoring it isn't the answer. Jesus knows that. She needs someone to forgive her and remove her sin, not just condemn her to have the rope of guilt around her neck for the rest of her life.

In *The Scarlet Letter*, Nathaniel Hawthorne shows insight into and empathy for his character, Hester Prynne, a woman in a Puritan

---

[236] John 8:5.

community found guilty of adultery. Part of her punishment includes wearing a red letter "A" on her chest for the rest of her life, reminding herself and others of her grievous act. One young wife and mother who observes Hester's attire says, "Let her cover the mark as she will, the pang of it will be always in her heart."[237] Another lady chides her neighbours for gossiping: "Not a stitch in that embroidered letter, but she has felt it in her heart."[238] Without a rescuer, the pang of our guilt will always be in our hearts, and Jesus understands that.

The test applied to Jesus through the accused woman in the biblical account doesn't turn out the way the pious men intend. Jesus isn't going to play their game, especially not at this woman's expense. He bends down and silently writes on the ground with his finger while they continue to bother him.[239] We have no clue what Jesus wrote, although people have speculated about it since the Bible was written. The result of his action is what's critical, not the words themselves, or they would appear in the text. Finally, Jesus stands up, looks at the pious men, and says, "*Let him who is without sin among you be the first to throw a stone at her.*" Then he goes back to his writing.[240]

Does she suck in her breath, wondering, *What now*? Does she attempt to keep her body as still as possible to remove any attention from herself because the focus is now on her accusers, and she desperately wants it to stay that way? At this point, she *wants* to be invisible. Saying it's a tense situation would be a gross understatement.

And then the tension begins to dissolve. One by one, the older men walk away.[241] The more years they've lived, the more transgressions they've racked up on their scorecards; thus, their hypocrisy exposed, they have nothing to say. The rest follow, each in turn.

Left alone with Jesus, the woman wonders what he will do. Her ultimate fate now rests in his hands. Slowly exhaling and trying to

....

[237] Hawthorne, *The Scarlet Letter*, 13.

[238] Hawthorne, *The Scarlet Letter*, 15.

[239] John 8:6.

[240] John 8:7–8.

[241] John 8:9.

bring her heartbeat under control, she awaits his verdict. Surprisingly, he doesn't immediately pass judgement but asks her a question: "What happened to all those men who brought you here? Hasn't even one of them stayed to condemn you?"[242] Cautiously, trembling, she answers, "No one, Lord."[243] *Can there be hope? Is it even remotely possible that I might survive this?*

And then Jesus delivers the words that set her free and change the course of her life forever. He tells her he doesn't condemn her either: *"Go, and from now on sin no more."*[244] This man, the highest religious authority, chooses to speak words of life to her. He could deliver her to the pious men to punish as they wish, but Jesus opts to pursue the woman and her needs and show her mercy rather than fulfilling the letter of the law. She is not invisible to him. He sees the broken, hurting person beneath the offence. And not only does he free her from her sin, but he releases her from the judgement of the men. Best of all, he welcomes her as a Beloved Daughter.

Jesus defines grace for us through his treatment of that dejected woman. He sees us, and when we deserve punishment for our actions, he forgives us and welcomes us as Beloved Daughters. I envision that woman walking away, stunned and in awe of the love and kindness she's just received. Wearing a big red letter "A" on her chest would never free her from the guilt and burden of her sin. Jesus removes that millstone from her and transforms her life.

Having been forgiven so much, I don't think she intends to return to her old ways. Jesus gives her a new beginning, not to live as before, but to follow a new direction in life. No longer a dead woman walking, she's now part of God's family, and she will love him forever after experiencing such grace and mercy.

....

[242] John 8:10 (paraphrased).

[243] John 8:11.

[244] John 8:11.

The women in these two narratives both experienced the grace of God through Jesus' words and actions. They began as invisible women, but he saw and loved them, ministered to their needs, and welcomed them as Beloved Daughters, regardless of the packages they were wrapped in. Sure, they were imperfect, fixer-upper, guilty, invisible women, but that makes their cases all the sweeter. After all, aren't we all in the imperfect, fixer-upper category one way or another?

Possibly something you've done haunts you and overshadows your admirable qualities, leaving you feeling shamed, unseen, and floundering. Like the pious men, the longer we have lived, the more times we have stumbled. But Jesus loves us and is still in the business of rescuing us. If we ask, he will forgive what we've done or who we were and liberate us from the cloud of our past shame that renders us invisible. The claws of the past no longer have a hold over us.

We can all revel in God's love as Beloved Daughters. There's an unlived future ahead, one of freedom and possibility, and he's willing to lead us through it. And if you haven't begun your journey yet, jump in. Your adventure awaits!

HE KNOWS YOUR NAME

Each woman we encountered in the previous chapters had a different story, but their endings were the same. God extended his love and grace to each invisible woman and treasured each one as a Beloved Daughter. And that made all the difference. Illness didn't thwart God, nor did infertility, a bad attitude, a terrible reputation, being a grouchy workaholic, or even immoral behaviour. Is there anything you'd like to add to the list? Whether from the Old Testament, before Jesus' time, or the New, while he walked the earth and after, each story reveals the tender heart of God and his love. He saw and pursued each woman. The details and situations vary, but God's love doesn't. He didn't discount their distress or suffering or offer stale clichés and tell them to get over it. He sent angels with a message to a few, healed the wombs and broken hearts of others, and to some, he spoke words that changed their lives. To each he gave hope—that is what God does.

That same God knows your name. To him, you're a unique and dearly loved individual. Your sin doesn't define you, nor does your job description. You don't have to wear a letter embroidered on your chest to tell the world the worst thing you've ever done. But conversely, you don't need to wear a T-shirt that lists your accomplishments to be appreciated and accepted either. He knows who you are. He knows your name, and he loves you.

The first five verses of Psalm 139 speak about how intimately God knows you:

> 1 O Lord, you have searched me and known me!
> 2 You know when I sit down and when I rise up;
> you discern my thoughts from afar.
> 3 You search out my path and my lying down
> and are acquainted with all my ways.
> 4 Even before a word is on my tongue,
> behold, O Lord, you know it altogether.
> 5 You hem me in, behind and before,
> and lay your hand upon me.

That isn't the description of a God so absorbed in partying with people in heaven that he's too busy to care about you. Nor is it the picture of a celestial ogre who occasionally takes delight as your life crashes and burns.

The God of the Bible is aware of every aspect of your life and "*chose* [you] *in him before the foundation of the world*."[245] He knows where you are at all times, what you're doing, and what you're likely to do. He even knows what you're thinking. That's a daunting thought, because you can't hide anything from him. But it's also comforting because, as with the ladies we studied, he knows the issues that cause you sleepless nights. And when you're overwhelmed by seemingly unsolvable problems, he knows that too.

You're not alone, because he surrounds you and keeps his hand on you. It's not a trap; it's a cocoon. God's love encompasses you, so you don't need to fret during those dark hours. Isaiah 43:1b–3 assures us:

---

[245] Ephesians 1:4.

Fear not, for I have redeemed you; *I have called you by name, you are mine.* When you pass through the waters, I will be with you; and through the rivers, they shall not overwhelm you; when you walk through fire you shall not be burned, and the flame shall not consume you. For I am the Lord your God, the Holy One of Israel, your Savior … (emphasis added)

Yes, he is. That promise covers every eventuality you're likely to face and then some. He's that big. And he loves you that much.

How can we be so sure? Jesus himself said, "*The sheep hear his voice* [referring to himself as the shepherd], *and he calls his own sheep by name* …"[246] Further along that passage, he says, "*I am the good shepherd. I know my own and my own know me.*"[247] To me, that's not just convincing; it makes me want to sob as if he were enveloping me in a hug so warm and comforting that life's hurts and uncertainties melt away in his presence. Deuteronomy 33:27a says, "*The eternal God is your refuge, and underneath are the everlasting arms*" (NIV). A giant hug.

There will be times along your journey when you don't feel like a Beloved Daughter. Feelings don't always reflect reality. Sometimes I feel I've failed because I don't meet my unrealistic expectations. When we doubt God loves or sees us, we must challenge that perception. Thoughts often influence our feelings, so we need to ask ourselves if our thoughts are true. The Bible says that God loves us and knows us intimately, so our reality is that we are Beloved Daughters and not invisible. Trust him and focus on that truth—your feelings will catch up. You are secure in him, and that's an excellent place to live.

---

[246] John 10:3b.

[247] John 10:14.

Let's review what we've learned from the lives of the ladies we've investigated. It's encouraging to see how God saw their hearts and changed their lives and to know that the same God loves and treasures us.

To the lady who'd been bleeding for twelve years, Jesus gave health and a new identity. She didn't give up, and Jesus didn't see her illness as permanent. He put everything else on hold while he pursued this determined woman. Her faith and his power released her from a life of invisibility and gave her a new reality. Not only was she well when she walked away, but Jesus affirmed her as a Daughter and blessed her too. If you struggle with a situation that you can't see any way to resolve, take a lesson from this lady and place it in God's hands. Psalm 9:10 gives us hope: "*Those who know your name put their trust in you, for you, O Lord, have not forsaken those who seek you.*"

Sarah felt invisible, forgotten by the God who'd promised her a son but didn't seem to follow through. So in her mind, the crazy notion of making God's plan happen without God's help somehow morphed into a brilliant idea. Not the wisest approach ever, but again, a relatable figure. How often have we run ahead of what God wants for us, only to create chaos that would have been avoided had we been patient? Although her plan backfired spectacularly, God pursued Sarah, fulfilled his promise to this Beloved Daughter, and honoured her faith forever by placing her in the Hall of Faith in Hebrews. Through her, we learn we're not invisible to God, even if we do idiotic things. And the good news is that he still cares for us and can use us, imperfections and all, to accomplish his purposes.

Hagar was a girl caught in a miserable situation, invisible as a person, just a functionary filling a role. Becoming a surrogate mother was not her choice, but she made things worse for herself. Who among us has never done something like that? Twice when she was alone and without a friend in the world, God sent an angel to her. He knew how that despondent soul felt, pursued her, and didn't wait until she had sorted out her life and become Little Miss Perfect before he cared for her as a Beloved Daughter. Learning is a process. Hagar didn't learn everything at once, and we don't either. There are no perfection awards on my wall, and I assume the same is true for you, but we can put our hope and trust in the same God who was there for Hagar. He didn't abandon her, and he won't abandon us. God's love is big and deep enough to encompass her and all of us, even if we've contributed to some of our own problems.

Rahab was an invisible lady hidden in the shadows, and she came with baggage. Previous experience as a prostitute isn't something we would consider an asset on a resume when applying to become an ancestor of the Saviour of the world. Fortunately, God thinks differently than we do. Rahab stepped outside the bounds of her world and acted with courage and faith to assist God's people. He pursued and rewarded this Beloved Daughter monumentally for her faith by placing her in the lineage of Jesus and in the Hall of Faith in Hebrews. It wasn't a label from her past that was important; it was her faith. We don't need to remain invisible in the shadows and fear that the shame of our past might disqualify us from impacting our world for God. Her heavenly Father saw and loved Rahab, baggage and all, and he sees and loves us too.

Naomi and Ruth were two widows at a time and in a culture where that meant poverty and invisibility. However, despite her losses, Naomi didn't turn away from God but lived in a way that drew her daughter-in-law Ruth to the God she served. Ruth loved Naomi and came to love the God she loved, and God loved them both. He saw, lovingly pursued, and took extraordinary measures to care for these Beloved Daughters. Their heavenly Father gave Ruth a husband from the bloodline needed to recover their land and produce an heir to carry on their family name. Best of all, the delighted groom dearly loved Ruth and her mother-in-law. Through their narratives, we learn that God sees our distress, and his love can penetrate undesirable places. Although our lives may take a trajectory we wouldn't willingly choose, God can use our unpleasant experiences in ways we could never foresee. Even when life is anything but promising, we can depend on him.

When the invisible Hannah—the woman who couldn't bear the children expected of a wife in her culture—connected with God, her life changed. Afterwards, she praised and worshipped him with a new focus rather than continuing to despair over what she didn't have. God pursued her and answered the prayer of this Beloved Daughter for a child, and even though it contained a costly promise on her part, she was joyful. This spiritual giant has much to teach us. Hannah didn't cling to her son tightly because she had waited for him for so long. Instead, what this lady desired most, she offered back to God, turned her focus to him, and praised him for who he was, despite her feelings. That is maturity. But even if we aren't at that level yet, through this story we learn more about the God who sees and pursues a desperate woman and hears her cry. He may not answer our prayers the same way he answered Hannah's, or even the way we might hope, but he will listen and reach out to us. He has a soft spot for his Beloved Daughters.

Leah and Rachel travelled a bumpy path from invisible to Beloved Daughters. Nevertheless, their lives speak of how God pursued each of these women and responded to their individual needs. Leah felt invisible because she longed for, but didn't receive, her husband's love. And although God didn't supernaturally change her husband's feelings, he saw this desolate soul and blessed her with a houseful of children to nurture and fill the gaping hole in her life. Rachel felt invisible because she longed for babies but was infertile. God ultimately granted this heartbroken woman's request, although sadly, she didn't live long to enjoy it. Like Leah and Rachel, God hasn't forgotten us and will support us in our difficulties. He may not fix things our way, or according to the schedule we set, but he is in control, loves us, and sees our misery as he did these sisters'. Trust him with the tough stuff. He is faithful.

Martha, the scullery maid, lost and invisible in the kitchen, was always bustling, but her priorities were confused. Mary was hidden in the background and, to her sister, appeared to be a slacker; however, she chose to use her time to learn from Jesus. And Jesus pursued the heart of each of these sisters and saw and loved them both. Their choices teach us the importance of periodic priority checks to ensure we spend our limited time and energy wisely. Through them, we also see that Jesus knows our burdens, but our responsibilities shouldn't preclude spending time with him. Service is important, but no matter how worthy it is, our relationship with him makes us his Beloved Daughters, not service or sacrifice.

The woman at the well and the adulterous woman are the final pair of this group. They weren't people you would likely follow as role models. Who they were was overshadowed by what they had done. But Jesus saw and loved them both and chose to reveal that he was the Messiah to one and forgive, rather than condemn, the other. He met them where they were; no credentials as paragons of virtue required. Both began their encounters with Jesus as invisible women and left as Beloved Daughters, filled with joy and excitement. Jesus can forgive whatever we've done and won't condemn us if we confess our sins and follow him. When he forgives us, he releases us to blossom, free from the burden of our guilt, and the claws of the past have no hold over us.

Our spiritual-growth journey will undoubtedly include numerous personalized lessons. These experiences will teach us more about the heart of God and our identity as Beloved Daughters. Will each challenge be the most fun we've ever had? Probably not. All we have to do is look at each of the women profiled in this book to see that life isn't a series of good times punctuated by vacations and festivities. If that were the case, we would never learn anything.

But see how their stories ended, each knowing she was a Beloved Daughter, seen, pursued, and loved by God. Isaiah 45:3 says, "*I will give you the treasures of darkness and the hoards in [riches stored in (NIV)] secret places, that you may know that it is I, the Lord, the God of Israel, who call you by your name.*" The dark places aren't the ones we long to experience, but they are where we find those hidden treasures and learn who he is. He knows our names, and he is in those places with us. Romans 8:38–39 says:

> For I am sure that neither death nor life, nor angels nor rulers, nor things present nor things to come, nor powers, nor height nor depth, nor anything else in all creation, will be able to separate us from the love of God in Christ Jesus our Lord.

So tuck that in your back pocket for the days you feel like Hagar, alone and wandering in the wilderness. Fortunately, we Daughters can hold one another's hands along the journey.

Knowing your identity, that you are a Beloved Daughter, isn't all about warm fuzzies. It's a beginning, not an end, because God has a deeper purpose than sorting out your feelings. The comfort that comes from understanding who you are is lovely, but the more critical element is the freedom that comes with that understanding.[248] When we finally grasp how much he loves us, he frees us from the lie that we're invisible, that we don't matter, and from the insecurities that plague us. That freedom releases us to do and be what God plans for us. That revelation in my life resulted in this book, and he will lead you on your own adventure. Ephesians 3:20 tells us, "[He] *is able to do immeasurably more than all we ask or imagine ...*" (NIV).

The Woman at the Well was set free and ran and told her entire community about Jesus, the Messiah. She was on fire! Your adventure won't be another "should" vying for your attention and time to add guilt and obligation to your life. When a life-transforming conviction burns within you, you want to share what Jesus did and can do because he did it for you. At the end of each of these women's tales is joy. How they got there differed and wasn't always the path they would have chosen, but in the end, they each found joy. It awaits you too.

We began this book with the story of my crash, when I felt like my life had deteriorated into the role of a scullery maid and that I was utterly invisible. My physical situation remains largely unchanged—my conditions are the same as before, and I still have to pace myself, picking and choosing activities to keep my busyness to a reasonable level to maintain my health. But something has changed. Today I see myself in a new light, with a new identity. I know I am more than what I do. Everyone in my world may still not see my essence, but I know God does, and I know that who I am as his Beloved Daughter is more important than how well I make sourdough bread. My Martha lessons are a work in progress, as is my life. There are still times when I'm frustrated by my limitations and feel less than I once was, but my position as a Beloved Daughter is secure and isn't affected by what I physically can or cannot do.

You have a heavenly Father who loves you and will continue to lead you. These words, penned more than a century and a half ago by Joseph Gilmore, still ring true today:

---

[248] Galatians 5:1.

He leadeth me! O blessed thought!
> O words with heavenly comfort fraught!
> Whate'er I do, where're I be,
> Still 'tis God's hand that leadeth me.
> He leadeth me, He leadeth me,
> By His own hand He leadeth me:
> His faithful follower I would be,
> For by His hand He leadeth me.[249]

He sees you. You are not invisible to him, and he will lead you along your journey. Philippians 1:6 says, "*And I am sure of this, that he who began a good work in you will bring it to completion at the day of Jesus Christ.*" Not only will he complete the project that is you, but he'll take you to some remarkable places while he does:

> The Sovereign Lord is my strength;
> he makes my feet like the feet of a deer,
> he enables me to tread on the heights.
> (Habakkuk 3:19, NIV)

So stand tall, take your place in his family, and see what he will do with your life, Beloved Daughter. Joy awaits.

---

[249] Gilmore, "He Leadeth Me," 368.

How to Become a Follower of Christ
and a Beloved Daughter

Each of us has sinned,[250] and the Bible doesn't give us a sliding scale for the severity of sin. No dividing line indicates which sins God winks at and which seal our eternal fate. Sin is sin, and we have all participated in it. And death is the penalty for sin.[251] We can never be good enough or work hard enough to save ourselves.[252] According to the book of Isaiah, "*all our righteous deeds are like a polluted garment.*"[253] Not a pretty picture.

Now the good news. God loved us so much "*that he gave his only Son, that whoever believes in him should not perish but have eternal life.*"[254]

....

[250] Romans 3:23.

[251] Romans 6:23.

[252] Ephesians 2:8–9.

[253] Isaiah 64:6.

[254] John 3:16.

God sent Jesus to rescue us while we were still sinners[255] because we had no other way out of the mess we'd created. Jesus died on the cross to take our punishment. To access his gift of eternal life,[256] he wants us to believe in him and choose to follow him.

Repeatedly, the Bible tells us to repent (e.g., Mark 1:15; 2 Peter 3:9), which in part means to be remorseful for our sins. But it's not merely feeling sorry for what we've done and modifying our behaviour. According to the *Holman Illustrated Bible Dictionary*, "repentance refers to a deeply seated and thorough turning from self to God,"[257] a change in direction. So when we confess our sins, believe, and put our faith in Jesus, he forgives us and gives us eternal life.[258] We don't confess to clear the slate so we may continue as before, only with a ticket to heaven now tucked into our back pocket. We believe in him and turn and follow him. That said, we will fail at times. We'll never be perfect on this side of heaven, but we can ask for his forgiveness when we fall short.

Faith is the basis of our relationship with Jesus; he is the Son of God and is worthy of that faith. He doesn't change,[259] so his promises are still valid. The essence of his message is: God gives us eternal life through Jesus;[260] when we repent and put our faith in him, we pass from death into life, eternally speaking, and he will no longer judge us for what we've done.[261] That's a nutshell worth treasuring.

I encourage you to take that step and cross the divide from death to life. Pray with me and begin your journey as a follower of Christ: "Dear God, I know I am a sinner, and I ask for Your forgiveness. I believe Jesus Christ is Your Son. I believe He died for my sin and that You raised Him to life. I want to trust Him as my Saviour and follow Him … from this

---

[255] Romans 5:8.

[256] Romans 6:23.

[257] Palmer, "Repentance," 1376.

[258] 1 John 1:9.

[259] Hebrews 13:8.

[260] 1 John 5:11.

[261] John 5:24.

day forward. Guide my life and help me to do Your will. I pray this in the name of Jesus. Amen."[262]

The Bible assures us that *"Whoever has the Son has life."*[263] Furthermore, Jesus promised to always be with us[264] and not forsake us.[265] So you're in good hands.

Do you know *"there is joy before the angels of God over one sinner who repents"*?[266] A party is happening in heaven right now on your behalf. That's exciting, Beloved Daughter!

Now go and tell someone and continue your walk of faith!

---

[262] Billy Graham Evangelical Assoc., "Begin Your Journey to Peace," para. 5.

[263] 1 John 5:12a.

[264] Matthew 28:20.

[265] Hebrews 13:5.

[266] Luke 15:10.

Let's Get Personal: Questions for Discussion or Reflection

If you'd like to delve further into the stories and ideas discussed in this book, these questions will assist you with self-reflection, group discussion, journaling, or sharing with someone you trust. Whichever is your preferred method, take some time to allow God to speak to you through the lives of these women. And as he did for Naomi and Ruth, he will work on creating a "prize-worthy botanical garden" from your life. Grow deep and strong, Beloved Daughter.

Introduction
1. When have you felt invisible, unseen? How did it affect your life?
2. What other feelings did you wrestle with during that period?
3. Did you eventually overcome those feelings? How?
4. In this Introduction, the author talks about reflecting on whether anyone really knew her *essence*. How would you describe the idea of the *essence* of a person? Do you have the sense of being known at that level?

5. The writer describes having a *God Moment* when she sensed she was hearing a message God specifically intended for her. Have you ever experienced such a *God Moment?* If so, describe its impact on you spiritually and on your actions.
6. What would you say to someone who feels invisible?

1. THE HEMORRHAGING WOMAN: MARK 5:21–34; LUKE 8:40–48; MATTHEW 9:20–22

1. Have you ever been sidelined for health issues or other reasons? What was the most difficult part of that period in your life? What positives or lessons did you gain from that experience that you may not have otherwise?
2. What do you think was the most challenging part of the hemorrhaging woman's situation?
3. What does having grit mean to you? When do you need to exercise courage, dig deeply, and find the grit to deal with something, and when do you need to ask for help?
4. What momentous before-and-after events have you experienced, aside from obvious ones such as graduation, marriage, the birth of a baby, etc.?
5. Have you ever received a blessing from someone that impacted your life? If you have, please describe it. What elements would you include in a blessing for someone in your world?
6. Have you ever returned to a community and had to reintegrate into life there? What helped you find your place again? Where did God fit into that situation for you?
7. What part of this story resonates with you the most?
8. What main lesson did you learn through exploring the story of the hemorrhaging woman?

2. Sarah:

Genesis 12:1–5, 15:1–6, 16:1–6, 17:15–21, 18:1–15, 21:1–12

1. How would you feel if your husband of many years decided you were going to pack up everything you own and move to a remote area? Knowing you were unlikely to ever have contact again with anyone from your former life aside from those in your group, how would you respond to his announcement?

2. What do you think your initial reaction would have been to the promise of a much-desired child when you were already on the far side of menopause?

3. What would you have done if the years had dragged by with no baby in sight even though God had promised you one, and you were much closer to death than your child-bearing years? At what point would you give in to despair, or how might you keep from falling into despair?

4. How would you react if you were listening at the tent door and learned you would have a child at ninety? When you were sure you were pregnant, what emotions would you experience?

5. Describe how you might have felt in Sarah's place when the servant you instructed to fill your role became haughty and treated you with contempt. Assuming the situation had become intolerable, what solution would you have chosen or at least seriously considered?

6. What would have been your most significant challenges as a mother raising this child on whose future so much rested?

7. The Bible ultimately places Sarah in the Hall of Faith in Hebrews. What sets her apart from others in the scriptures who also had faith but aren't listed there?

8. What part of Sarah's narrative gives you the most hope?

3. HAGAR:
GENESIS 16:1–16, 21:8–21

1. Having read Hagar's story, what are your thoughts about her conscription into the role of a surrogate mother—a position she didn't choose? Do you feel empathy with her or exasperation that she contributed, in large part, to her own mess? Something else?

2. Have you ever felt completely and utterly alone with nowhere to turn? How did you get through it?

3. How would you respond if an angel appeared and offered you a personal message from God? In what ways does God speak to you?

4. The angel told Hagar to return home and submit to her mistress. Our human tendency is to rebel against restrictions we don't like. How do we learn to submit to authorities even if we disagree—assuming the directive doesn't contradict what scripture teaches?

5. If God told you your unborn son's future would look like Ishmael's, what thoughts and emotions would surge through you? How would that knowledge affect your parenting?

6. Hagar placed her child under a tree when she was out of options and left him to die. In her place, what would you do if you felt unable to meet your child's needs?

7. Can you think of a time when God helped you in an unusual way amid great difficulty (e.g., money suddenly arrived in the mail, someone unexpectedly showed up to help, etc.)? If God has come to your rescue in an unexpected and perfectly timed way, please describe it.

8. What part of Hagar's story strengthens your faith in the God who saw and loved her?

4. RAHAB:
JOSHUA 2, 6

1. How do we use invisibility as a cloak to hide from other people and even God?

2. Suppose Rahab, the prostitute awaiting deliverance, walked into your church, and the congregation only knew her reputation but not her faith story. How would she feel in that setting? How can we make all people, the Rahabs and others, comfortable in our faith community—our church, small groups, etc.? Would someone from the streets be accepted in our company? How do we get beyond our comfort zone and not create an "us and them" situation?

3. How do you think Rahab developed the faith in God that she evidenced?

4. Could you have been courageous enough to take the stand Rahab did? Why or why not?

5. How would you have held on to your faith while crammed in a small home with numerous relatives and the Israelite army on the march?

6. How do you think Rahab would have been received in the Israelite community after the fall of Jericho? As a heroine? An outsider who wormed her way in by a fortuitous act and nothing more? Something else?

7. In what ways do labels, whether given by others or ourselves, prevent us from fully embracing our identity as Beloved Daughters? Or do they—why or why not?

8. What lesson from this story can you apply to your life?

5. RUTH AND NAOMI:
RUTH 1–4

1. Have you ever moved far from your family and old friends? What challenges did you face, and how did you adjust?

2. Have you ever lost a spouse or a close family member? What do you remember being the hardest part of the experience? Did you feel invisible? What helped you cope? Where did God fit into your grieving process?

3. What feelings might you experience if you were saying a final farewell to the town where all your close family members lay buried, and you wouldn't likely ever return?

4. What ramifications do you think Ruth considered before pledging to stay with Naomi? Do you think she had second thoughts when they arrived in Bethlehem, homeless and jobless?

5. In twenty-first-century Western culture, our emphasis is on independence. Consider how Ruth willingly trusted Naomi's advice and direction. What lessons can we learn from their relationship, despite living in a different era and society?

6. How would you have reacted to Boaz's revelation that he was second in line as a redeemer? The author states that Ruth "leaves the problem with Boaz, prudently aware of what is within her control and what is not. Then, she lets God do the rest." When you can't control the outcome, what steps can you take to build trust in God?

7. Describe a hard place in your life where God came through and proved himself faithful when the road ahead looked bleak. What lesson did you learn then that you might not have learned if life had carried along merrily?

8. What resonates the most with you in the story of these two women, and what is your takeaway?

6. Hannah:
1 Samuel 1:1–2:21

1. What challenges might you encounter in Hannah's place if your culture highly valued motherhood and you couldn't bear children?
2. How would you cope with a situation like Hannah's, where you know your annual "vacation" would be a fractious and miserable endurance test?
3. Have you ever dared to pray a dangerous prayer that would be costly to you if answered? What was the result?
4. When Hannah prayed for a son and promised to return him to God if he granted her request, she didn't know the end of the story. Describe a time when you prayed for something and God answered in a way far beyond your expectations.
5. What struggles do you think Hannah faced as the time approached to relinquish her son's care to others so he could fulfill his service? As our faith grows and we learn more about the faithfulness of God, as Hannah did, how do our struggles change, or do they?
6. Why do you think God sometimes allows us to travel a difficult path? Does the why matter while you're experiencing hardship? How do we learn to leave the why with God and trust him with life's unknowns?
7. Have you reached a place where you can praise God even during tough times? If so, what helped you get to that point?
8. What part of Hannah's story speaks to you and why?

7. LEAH AND RACHEL:
GENESIS 27:41–45, 28:1–2, 29:1–35, 30:1–24,
35:16–18, 49:31

1. Is Leah a relatable character for you? Have you ever felt you lived in the shadow of someone more beautiful than you, or smarter, or who got all the breaks in life? If so, how did you deal with it?

2. How do you think Leah felt when Jacob realized she was his bride, not Rachel, and rejected her the morning after her wedding? How would you have reacted?

3. What feelings and challenges do you imagine Leah experienced a week into her married life when her sister entered the union as the sought-after wife?

4. What do you think Rachel considered as her wedding approached, knowing she was entering the marriage as the second wife and would have to share Jacob with Leah forever?

5. How have you learned to cope with a problematic ongoing situation?

6. As the years passed, Rachel realized Leah was Jacob's baby factory, and having offspring wasn't looking hopeful for her. With our constant access to social media, consider how comparison with and jealousy of others can make us feel dissatisfied with our lives and even question our worth. What are the ramifications for other areas of our lives if we fall into this trap of comparison and the resulting negative spiral? What steps can we take to redirect our gaze and appreciate what God has done for us and the gifts he has given us?

7. Repeatedly we read that God saw Leah's heart. Later, he also remembered Rachel and answered her prayer. How does that knowledge impact you, and how does it relate to your life?

8. What else have you learned from Leah and Rachel that you can apply to yourself?

8. MARTHA AND MARY
LUKE 10:38–42; JOHN 11:1–44, 12:1–8

1. Is Martha or Mary the more relatable character in this story for you? Why?

2. Have you ever thought Martha had a good reason to complain about Mary? If so, what's your conclusion now?

3. Someone still had to perform the daily domestic chores at the three siblings' home after Jesus left. Since that seemed to be Martha's domain, how do you think her day-to-day life changed after her encounter with Jesus?

4. If Jesus had come when summoned, what lessons do you think Martha and Mary might have missed had Lazarus not died? How do we sometimes waste opportunities for growth amid difficulties?

5. Reflect on the concept of giving an extravagant gift to God as Mary did when people in need are suffering. How do we decide the best way to use our limited resources?

6. Devotion and service are indispensable, but how do you find the right mix? How do you balance the shoulds and have-tos in life with more important things?

7. What part of this study of two sisters and their different choices impacts you the most and why?

8. Everyone's pathway to Christ is unique and important. Reflect on how Jesus came into your life. If you're still on your journey of decision, consider how God transformed these women's lives and the difference it made for them. May you embrace the love of the heavenly Father as he whispers your name and calls you to himself through a relationship with his son, Jesus.

9. THE WOMAN AT THE WELL AND THE ADULTEROUS WOMAN: JOHN 4, 8:1–11

1. What would your reaction be if a stranger told you everything you'd ever done? (Assuming there was no social media or any other way someone could humanly know those things.)
2. If you struggle with seeing obstacles when you need to exercise faith, how do you overcome that tendency?
3. Why do you think Jesus revealed his identity to the woman at the well? Why not the mayor of the town or a prominent religious leader?
4. If you knew your reputation in your community wasn't stellar, like the woman at the well, how would you respond after learning who Jesus was? Run and tell the world, or enjoy your cherished memory and try to remain in obscurity? Why?
5. Place yourself in the position of the woman being hauled out of her tent by the morality police. What thoughts would be racing through your mind?
6. Have you ever been in a position like the accused woman, where your long-term survival was uncertain? Did you talk to God? How were those prayers different from your usual ones when life was more predictable? What became important to you during that period, and what did not? Has it had a lasting influence on your day-to-day life?
7. After the adulterous woman left Jesus' presence, free from guilt and shame, what do you think she did? Slink home quietly and hope no one noticed? Run and tell the neighbours who saw her arrested about what happened? Seek out her partner that got away (and do what)? Other options?
8. What insights have you gained from either or both of these women's stories? What can you apply to your life?

10. He Knows Your Name

1. Of the stories that we studied, which one do you relate to the most? If more than one impacts you (hopefully that's the case!), pick one and explain why it speaks to you.

2. How is God's hand upon us like a cocoon, not a trap?

3. When doubts arise in your life and you don't feel like a Beloved Daughter, or you forget that you are one and seem lost in the chaos of life, how do you get back on track? How do you remind yourself or hold on to the fact that he knows your name and loves you with an everlasting love (Jeremiah 31:3)?

4. The writer says, "God has a purpose [for your life] far deeper than purely sorting out your feelings." How do you respond to that statement?

5. What scripture verses or passages have helped you during difficult periods of your life?

6. "Freedom is not an end in itself," the author writes. The freedom she experienced, resulting from understanding her place in God's family, set her on the path to writing this book. Is God stirring something in your heart that you want to explore as you move forward in his freedom?

7. Our journey with God is a winding road with many bumps, and it doesn't always unfold as planned. No matter what the issue is in your life, others have been there too. If you're struggling with something, is there someone you trust with whom you can talk? If this is a new area of vulnerability for you, requesting her prayer support may be a way to begin. As a Beloved Daughter, remember that you are not an only child, and you have a Father who loves you dearly.

Now that you understand who you are, Beloved Daughter, embrace the freedom that knowledge brings, and see what God will do in your life!

References

Alighieri, Dante. *The Divine Comedy.* The Harvard Classics, Vol. 20. Translated by Henry F. Cary. New York, NY: P.F. Collier & Son, 1909–14; Bartleby.com, 2001. https://www.bartleby.com/20/. Accessed July 27, 2020.

Austin, Benjamin M. "Booths, Feast of." In The Lexham Bible Dictionary, edited by John D. Barry et al. Bellingham, WA: Lexham Press, 2016. Electronic edition, Logos Bible Software.

Billy Graham Evangelical Association. "Start Your New Life With Jesus." *Peace With God.* Billy Graham Evangelical Association [n.d.]. https://peacewithgod.net/. Accessed August 10, 2020.

Block, Daniel Isaac. *Judges, Ruth.* The New American Commentary, Vol. 6. Nashville: Broadman & Holman Publishers, 1999. Electronic edition, Logos Bible Software.

Canadian Oxford Dictionary, ed. Katherine Barber, 2nd ed. Don Mills: Oxford University Press, 2004.

Eisenberg, Ronald L. "Levirate Marriage and Halitzah: Ancient Customs Involving a Childless Widow." *My Jewish Learning.* https://www.myjewishlearning.com/article/levirate-marriage-and-halitzah. Accessed June 16, 2023.

Farber, Zev. "How Is It Possible that Jacob Mistakes Leah for Rachel?" *TheTorah.com,* 2017. https://www.thetorah.com/article/how-is-it-possible-that-jacob-mistakes-leah-for-rachel. Accessed October 15, 2020.

Franklin, Chase J. "Nazarite." In *The Lexham Bible Dictionary*, edited by John D. Barry et al. Bellingham, WA: Lexham Press, 2016. Electronic edition, Logos Bible Software.

Gilmore, Joseph. "He Leadeth Me." In *Hymns of Glorious Praise*, 368. Springfield, MO: Gospel Publishing House, 1969.

Guzik, David. "Genesis 29—Jacob's Marriages and Children." In *Enduring Word Bible Commentary*. https://enduringword.com/bible-commentary/genesis-29. Accessed June 16, 2023.

Guzik, David. "Leviticus 25—Special Sabbaths and Jubilees." In *Enduring Word Bible Commentary*. https://enduringword.com/bible-commentary/leviticus-25 https://enduringword.com/bible-commentary/leviticus-25. Accessed June 16, 2023.

Guzik, David. "Ruth 3—Ruth Makes an Appeal." In *Enduring Word Bible Commentary*. https://enduringword.com/bible-commentary/ruth-3. Accessed June 16, 2023.

Hawthorne, Nathaniel. *The Scarlet Letter*. Pleasantville, NY: The Reader's Digest Association, 1984.

Hess, Richard S. *Joshua: An Introduction and Commentary*. Tyndale Old Testament Commentaries, Vol. 6. Downers Grove, IL: InterVarsity Press, 1996. Electronic edition, Logos Bible Software.

Howard, David M. Jr. *Joshua*. The New American Commentary, Vol. 5. Nashville, TN: Broadman & Holman Publishers, 1998. Electronic edition, Logos Bible Software.

Kaiser, Henry J. as quoted in United States Congress. "Congressional Record: Proceedings and Debates of the United States Congress," Volume 113, Part 18 (19 March 2013) 24155. https://www.govinfo.gov/app/details/GPO-CRECB-1967-pt18/GPO-CRECB-1967-pt18-3-2. Accessed September 21, 2020.

Lewis, C.S. *The Lion, the Witch and the Wardrobe*. London, UK: HarperCollins,1992.

Long, V. Philips. *1 and 2 Samuel: An Introduction and Commentary*, edited by David G. Firth. In Tyndale Old Testament Commentaries, Vol. 3. Downers Grove, IL: IVP Academic: An Imprint of InterVarsity Press, 2020. Electronic edition, Logos Bible Software.

Matthews, K.A. *Genesis 11:2–50:26*. The New American Commentary, Vol. 1b. Nashville, TN: Broadman & Holman Publishers, 2005. Electronic edition, Logos Bible Software.

Matthews, Victor Harold, et al. *The IVP Bible Background Commentary: Old Testament*, Downers Grove, IL: InterVarsity Press, 2000. Electronic edition, Logos Bible Software, Dt 25:5–10.

Morris, Leon. *Luke: An Introduction and Commentary*. Tyndale New Testament Commentaries, Vol. 3. Dowers Grove: Intervarsity Press, 1988. Electronic edition, Logos Bible Software.

Myers, Allen C. "Dowry." In *The Eerdmans Bible Dictionary*. Grand Rapids, MI: Eerdmans, 1987. Electronic edition, Logos Bible Software.

Palmer, Clark. "Repentance." In *Holman Illustrated Bible Dictionary*, edited by Chad Brand et al. Nashville, TN: Holman Bible Publishers, 2003. Electronic edition, Logos Bible Software.

Peterson, Eugene H. *The Message*. Colorado Springs: NavPress, 2018.

Reimer, Rob. *Soul Care: Seven Transformational Principles for a Healthy Soul*. Franklin, TN: Carpenter's Son Publishing, 2016.

"Religions—Judaism: Sukkot," BBC. October 2011. https://www.bbc.co.uk/religion/religions/judaism/holydays/sukkot_1.shtml. Accessed June 16, 2023.

Rich, Tracey R. "The Role of Women." Judaism 101. https://www.jewfaq.org/women.htm. Accessed June 16, 2023.

Satlow, Michael. "Reconsidering the Rabbinic Ketubah Payment." In *The Jewish Family in Antiquity*, edited by Shaye J.D. Cohen, 133–52. Brown Judaic Studies, 2020. https://doi.org/10.2307/j.ctvzgb9cp.10. Accessed October 2, 2020.

Schmidt, Karen, illus. *The Gingerbread Man*. New York, NY: Scholastic Inc., 1985.

Steinmann, Andrew E. *Genesis: An Introduction and Commentary*. The Tyndale Commentary Series, Vol. 1. London, UK: InterVarsity Press, 2019. Electronic edition, Logos Bible Software.

The NET Bible First Edition Notes, "Genesis 29:17, 23." Richardson, TX: Biblical Studies Press, 2006. Electronic edition, Logos Bible Software.

"Timeline from Abraham to Exodus." *Harp's Crossing Baptist Church*, PDF (April 2014). https://www.harpscrossing.com/wp-content/uploads/2014/04/Timeline-From-Abram-to-Exodus.pdf. Accessed June 16, 2023.

Vincent, Noel. "Concept of Goel: Kinsmen-Redeemer." *Apologia Veritas: Defending Truth Blog*. December 10, 2007. http://apologiaveritas.org/2007/12/10/concept-of-goel-kinsman-redeemer/. Accessed June 16, 2023.

Woods, Edward J. *Deuteronomy: An Introduction and Commentary*, edited by David G. Firth. Tyndale Old Testament Commentaries, Vol. 5. Nottingham: Inter-Varsity Press, 2011. Electronic edition, Logos Bible Software.

Yeats, W.B. "Aedh Wishes for the Cloths of Heaven." In *The Wind Among the Reeds*. New York, NY: John Lane, 1899. https://archive.org/details/windamongreeds00yeat/page/60/mode/2up?ref=ol&view=theater. Accessed June 23, 2022.

Zimmerman, Jack. "Sukkot, The Feast of Booths (Known to Some as the Feast of Tabernacles)." *Jewish Voice Blog*. Jewish Voice Ministries Canada. December 1, 2015. https://www.jewishvoice.org/read/blog/sukkot-feast-booths-known-some-feast-tabernacles. Accessed June 16, 2023.

ACKNOWLEDGEMENTS

This book is my first, and while it represents a lifetime's experience in the making, the actual production time was much shorter. Therefore, any errors are mine alone. Any beauty, truth, and strength in the book, however, owe much to the contributions of others. My heartfelt thanks go to:

Nancy Loveless, who has walked with me through this project since its inception. Your prayers, support, enthusiasm, feedback, and insights have contributed greatly to this work. Thank you, my friend.

Patricia Paddey, copy editor, mentor, and friend. You shared your time and expertise and answered questions that helped a beginner navigate a world that seemed overwhelming. This book was indeed a team effort. You have modelled generosity for me on a plane I've never before experienced, and I am humbled and grateful. I bless you, dear friend.

Linda Gibson, who waded through the "litter box" version of the manuscript and offered helpful feedback, expertise, and encouragement. Thank you, Linda, for taking the time to help a friend during such a busy season in your own life.

Ana Wilton, who has loved me forever and has been a cheerleader through this entire process. Thank you, Ana, for your encouragement and prayers, and for spending hours checking Bible references.

Lois Holland, a dear friend, who has faithfully prayed for me throughout the project. You listened and offered wisdom at moments when I needed it the most. Thank you, Lois.

Kerry Wilson, for editing the final draft, polishing it and encouraging me along the way. Thank you, Kerry.

The ladies who openly shared their difficult experiences with me. You know who you are, and I thank you for entrusting me with pieces of your soul so other women may benefit. May the Lord reward you for your vulnerability and generosity.

My family and friends, for your love and support, especially prayer support, and for graciously understanding my need to work and allowing me the time to do so.

My husband and friend, Peter, who believed in me from the beginning. You pitched in and helped with many tasks formerly in my purview while I typed away, and you did so with grace and patience. You spent the pandemic lockdown largely alone and bored while I hid away and worked, never complaining when I couldn't come out and play. Thank you, Peter; I love you.

Most importantly, I thank the Lord for his faithfulness to me, his Beloved Daughter.

> I will sing of the Lord's great love forever;
>> with my mouth I will make your faithfulness known
>> through all generations.
> I will declare that your love stands firm forever ...
> (Psalm 89:1–2, NIV)

ABOUT THE AUTHOR

Brenda Erb Roberts and her husband, Peter, live near Georgian Bay in Ontario, Canada. Faith, family, and friends form the bedrock of her life, and their grandchildren add the sparkle. Brenda honed her story-telling gift by teaching children at her church for many years. She delights in using contemporary language and humour to reimagine stories from the Bible, making their lessons fresh for today's readers. Her English literature degree and Bible college training assist her in looking deeply into the scriptures and exploring their truths. Please visit: brendaerbroberts.com.